Howard examines how one's screenplay can be a ̣ provides an invaluable guide to maximizing your own world-building. An essential reference for any writer looking to create his or her own fictional mythology. Highly recommended.

— Stefan Blitz, Editor-in-Chief, Forces of Geek

Make Your Story Really Stinkin' Big is not only an accessible primer for writers, but it also clearly articulates a process by which professionals can implement transmedia storytelling techniques to elevate their projects. Houston Howard's humorous and enthusiastic vision is a worthy resource for anyone wanting to reach a wider audience with their work.

— Ian Puente, Vice President of Business Development and General Counsel at Samuel Goldwyn Films

These transmedia storytelling techniques are invaluable for every type of story. Indeed, Houston Howard's discussion of high concept, and analysis of story setting, are worth the price of admission alone. And there's much, much more. Read on. Write on.

— John L. Geiger Co-author, *Creativity & Copyright*

Yes, Houston Howard's book walks you through architecting your world, structuring your narrative, and all that other good stuff. But the best part of *Make Your Story Really Stinkin' Big* is that it's so packed with cool ideas, new ways of engaging audiences and exploring stories, it makes you want to quit reading and just go make stuff!

— Chad Gervich, Writer/Producer: *Dog with a Blog*, *After Lately*, *Wipeout*; Author: *Small Screen, Big Picture*

Make Your Story Really Stinkin' Big is a comprehensive guide to building transmedia worlds that last. From inception and creation to marketing and building communities that will support your franchise in the long run, this book is an insightful step-by-step guide for anyone looking to tell stories for entertainment or for branding in the twenty-first century.

— Christine Weitbrecht, Brand Consultant and Transmedia Producer; Editor of Thoughts on the T

Make Your Story Really Stinkin' Big urges you to roll up your sleeves and start thinking in new ways. Houston Howard not only gives you the tools to make your story "flow," but also passionately empowers you to get off your butt and do it! I give this book a stinkin' big recommendation — a must for any storyteller, regardless of whether you're writing a fragmented tale over a strategic host of platforms or are simply starting out in storytelling.

— Alison Norrington, Author, Playwright, Journalist, and Founder of storycentralDIGITAL

If you read just one screenwriting book a year, this year you should read Houston Howard's *Make Your Story Really Stinkin' Big*. Howard understands both the art and the craft, and he lets the reader dream about building a legacy, which is why most of us write.

— Mary J. Schirmer, Screenwriter-Producer; www.screenplayers.net

As an educator, I was thrilled to see absolutely all of my students, with all learning styles, completely engaged in the strategy Houston Howard presents in *Make Your Story Really Stinkin' Big*. Writing came to life in my classroom like never before. I now have students trying to get into my classes because they want to be part of our writing project. Howard's writing process is now a permanent part of my curriculum.

— Cari Rucker, English Teacher, Boyd County High School, Ashland, KY

Houston Howard's *Make Your Story Really Stinkin' Big* is the best introduction to the concept of transmedia storytelling that I have read. Even better, his thoughts for best practice are completely hands-on, readily understandable, and — for us writers — a lot of fun. I've already incorporated some of his ideas into my own current project, and it's better for it. If you only read one new book on cross-platform content creation this year, this should be it.

— Carey Martin, Screenwriter and Professor, Liberty University

I was absolutely amazed to see how the creative process Houston Howard sets forth in his book, *Make Your Story Really Stinkin' Big*, took my small children's book and rapidly expanded it into a viable franchise without sacrificing its creative integrity. In fact, it actually allowed me to explore areas of my story I didn't even realize were there! If you're a fiction author and want your story to last, you need to read this book.

— Nelson Gassman, Author of *The Sock Circus*

Reading *Make Your Story Really Stinkin' Big* will give you the upper hand in this cutthroat business. As a film marketing professional, I am confident that Houston Howard's forward thinking will change the way we create, market, and view entertainment. From the script stage, to multi-platform distribution, and beyond — do yourself a favor and explore the world that this book has to offer.

— Evan Colfer, Film Marketing Professional and Editor

As a marketing professional, I found Houston Howard's *Make Your Story Really Stinkin' Big* a refreshing new approach to storytelling, effective advertising, and promotions on just about any level. Advertising is about message delivery and, though its roots are in entertainment, this book explains how to create and deliver those messages to a variety of targets in their own environment. Truly an innovative approach as the industry moves into a more mixed-media environment.

— Jason Hager, Brand and Marketing Expert, The Manahan Group

Houston lays out a fantastic and easy-to-understand introduction to the future of media in *Make Your Story Really Stinkin' Big*. I was blown away by his helpful advice on preparing and building a storyworld that can expand your reach through multiple platforms and audiences. If you think transmedia is just retelling your same story in different media formats you are going to miss the future.

— Brian Godawa, Screenwriter: *To End All Wars*; Author: *Hollywood Worldviews*; and Novelist, *Chronicles of the Nephilim*

Make Your Story Really Stinkin' Big has given me answers to unanswered questions and expanded on my own experience and knowledge of creating a marketable product with the story in your head. No more guesswork and wasting time and money. You have arrived at the motherload of time-saving, money-sparing, and sanity-salvaging information.

— Charity Parenzini, Writer, Telly Award-winning Producer

Finally! No more tidbits of truths scattered here and there sending you on endless searches and pass/fail experiences. Houston Howard has delivered a treasure chest of information on what to do, how to do it, and where to take it from here.

— Mark Kudlow, Veteran Screenwriter

Houston Howard has provided an everyman's guidebook on how writers can "grow" their story and characters and expand their creative universe. Whether your starting point is a comic book, novel, song, game, television series, play, or film script, Howard provides helpful markers and exercises to map out your project to its fullest potential.

— Kathie Fong Yoneda, consultant, workshop leader, author of *The Script-Selling Game (2nd edition)*

MAKE

YOUR STORY

REALLY STINKIN' BIG

*How to go from concept to franchise and
make your story last for generations*

HOUSTON HOWARD

Published by Michael Wiese Productions
12400 Ventura Blvd. #1111
Studio City, CA 91604
tel. 818.379.8799
fax 818.986.3408
mw@mwp.com
www.mwp.com

Cover design: Johnny Ink www.johnnyink.com
Interior design: Gina Mansfield Design
Copy editor: Gary Sunshine

Printed by McNaughton & Gunn, Inc., Saline, Michigan
Manufactured in the United States of America

Library of Congress Cataloging-in-Publication Data

Howard, Houston, 1979-
 Make your story really stinkin' big : how to go from concept to franchise and make your story last for generations / Houston Howard.
   pages cm.
 ISBN 978-1-61593-155-2 (pbk.)
1. Motion picture authorship. 2. Motion picture plays--Technique. I.
Title.
 PN1996.H733 2013
 808.2'3--dc23
                          2013016168

Printed on recycled stock
Publisher plants ten trees for every one tree used to produce this book.

CONTENTS

ACKNOWLEDGMENTS

Thanks, God, for giving me access to Your matchless creativity. You did me a solid and I greatly appreciate it.

For understanding my long hours on my laptop, I'd like to thank my wife, Courtney. Coolest. Wife. Ever.

Also, thanks to my parents who have always encouraged me to follow my dreams.

Thanks to my One 3 Productions team for your trust and for helping me harness a seemingly impossible creative vision. Iron definitely sharpens iron.

WHY YOU SHOULD
READ
THIS BOOK

At this point, you're probably wondering why you should spend a portion of your hard-earned paycheck on this book. Maybe you're trying to decide between this book and another industry book? Or possibly you're considering saving the cash and going on a Red Box binge this weekend instead?

Listen, I love Red Box binges as much as the next guy, but honestly you should opt for the book. Why? Because all the things you'll learn from it are things I wish I would have known when I first began pursuing entertainment as a career.

You see, I graduated from law school on the East Coast. So, when I moved to Los Angeles to start producing and writing, I had two choices: go to film school and take on another $40,000 in student loans or figure out how to do it on my own.

I chose Door Number Two.

For the first couple of years, I read every Michael Wiese book I could afford. Seriously, I read at least twenty; it was like my own little film school, but with a $39,600 discount. However, even with my self-taught knowledge, I still needed a way to set myself apart from the seemingly 14 zillion uber-talented people trying to break into the industry at the same time.

I needed a way to do what I love, keep up with our ever-changing entertainment landscape, and, at the same time, be successful on my own terms.

So, I figured out a way to do it.

And you've guessed it... all the secrets, tips, tricks, and strategies are in this book.

FOREWORD

BY ROBERT PRATTEN

360° Storyweaving — or what the PGA defines as transmedia storytelling — is more than the meme of the moment. It's an essential way to attract and retain audiences and consumers. With this book it also becomes a methodical approach to maximizing the business potential of any creative idea.

In 2000, I quit work as a telecoms marketing consultant and went to film school. Eight years later and with two indie features to my name I discovered transmedia storytelling and realized instantly this was the industry's salvation. Music, movies, and books had all been ravaged by online file sharing and an explosion of user-generated content. This same seismic shift in media consumption and production had affected advertising, too — making it harder for the seller's message to reach buyers and easier for potential buyers to dodge and ignore advertising. I realized early on there would be a sweet spot for myself at the intersection of entertainment, marketing, and technology: using transmedia storytelling to blur the boundary of entertainment and marketing and using technology to connect all the parts.

In June 2012, I met with the author, Houston Howard, at the Bergamont Café in Los Angeles on a typically Californian warm, bright morning. We'd met to discuss possible areas of collaboration and cooperation with each an admirer of the other's work. When Houston told me he was writing a book to capture and share the knowledge he'd gained in developing transmedia franchises I immediately asked to read it. How could I have known, however high my expectations, that once I had it in my hands I would be totally blown away!

Make Your Story Really Stinkin' Big is an essential book for anyone working in the creative industries and by far the best of the transmedia books on the market at the time of this writing.

On first reading I found the book to be a real page-turner. I know that's a clichéd phrase but it's seldom used to describe a reference book. But with each passing chapter I was eager to know more, eager to learn Houston's perspective on how to leverage the most from a story, and eager to see how he'd approached the job of structuring a fully-fledged franchise and built a coherent storyworld. I devoured the book in two sittings and immediately emailed Houston to tell him he'd written the book the industry needed someone to write! A practical guidebook.

And so what I love most about this book are the lists, the breakdowns, the A-Z steps and the bullet points. It's a go-to practical reference book I've returned to many times even before it's been published. (Such as my privileged position as a reviewer has allowed me!)

While there are a growing number of people analyzing works of transmedia and providing us all with valuable and much needed insight, few offer practical how-to advice on how to set off in the right direction and how to improve what may already be in place. Maybe this is why Houston and I get along so well? We both have a desire to encourage others to get started and we endeavor to show how that might be done.

My own work is less about developing transmedia franchises and more about audience participation — applying storytelling and game mechanics to create dynamic, personalized experiences much like Alternate Reality Games (ARGs) and location-based stories. I apply this to storyworlds to create a layer of social participation that binds all the various platforms — books, videos, toys, and so on. When used with a franchise, the participation aspect is usually thought of as part of the marketing.

It was while working on a movie project in which I was tasked to build audience participation through social media and email that I first read *Make Your Story Really Stinkin' Big*. The section titled "Segments and Ladders" immediately grabbed my attention and started a series of discussions with the scriptwriter. Not only would the script be better for creating hierarchies in the two warring factions but it would give me additional material to work with. Relatively painless changes to the script were in fact made, opening up a whole host of new possibilities for a social game with better achievements, levels, and personalization. And the two platforms — feature film ("the entertainment") and social game ("the marketing") — were now much more tightly bound to the same storyworld and both were better for it.

The potential impact of *Make Your Story Really Stinkin' Big* on the reader's work should not be underestimated. The book is full of useful tips and checklists that allow the creator the best possible foundation for expanding and maximizing the business potential of his or her story.

This truly is my go-to book on transmedia story development!

. . . .

Robert Pratten is a feature film director, the founder of Transmedia Storyteller, and an expert on interactive, social, and pervasive cross-platform entertainment and marketing.

A FEW THINGS
TO GET
OUT OF THE WAY

WHO IS THIS BOOK FOR ANYWAY?

This book is for any professional, amateur, or would-be storyteller. You might be a novelist, comic writer, toy maker, producer, game designer, screenwriter, playwright, or transmedia enthusiast — anyone who is looking to get much more out of a story.

You want your story to be bigger? You want to position your story for mainstream engagement and commercial success? Then, whatever your creative title, this book will help you move in that direction.

WHO THE HECK IS THIS GUY?

Simply put, I'm the Co-Founder and Chief Storyteller of One 3 Productions — a collection of diverse creative professionals committed to telling stories that cause positive changes in people's lives.

There's work and there's your calling.

A calling is the kind of work that never actually feels like work. The kind of work you'd never compromise on. That you'd sacrifice for. The kind of work that has your fingerprints all over it and adds up to something. Something big. Something that couldn't happen anywhere else or with any other group of people.

That's the kind of work we do at One 3 Productions.

We've assembled a team made of music producers, board game designers, screenwriters, editors, directors, marketing professionals, comic writers, actors, and singers who all understand the times in which they live and are committed to using their combined talents to tell powerful stories that leave an endurable mark on today's culture.

We have a threefold approach to our business:

1. We develop original intellectual properties (IPs) with the focus and intent of producing the projects independently as transmedia franchises;

2. We develop original transmedia-ready IPs with the intent of shopping the project for acquisition or license from a studio partner or another entity; *and*

3. We consult with other content creators on the best way to diversify and grow their projects to have maximum commercial and mainstream impact.

With all three of these aspects, we use a comprehensive campaign approach, which we've coined *360° Storyweaving*. An optimum 360° Storyweaving Campaign includes three distinct phases:

1. *The Creation Phase*, where we create and design the story components around an original concept;

2. *The Immersion Phase*, where we design and plan marketing support for the story components through thematic merchandising and media blurring; *and*

3. *The Community Phase*, where we build communities through online engagement and interactivity as well as implement social outreach, which springs from the original purpose and theme of the project.

As a side note, this book is geared mainly toward the Creation Phase, which will deal with creatively developing the story concepts around the original concept and IP, which we consider to be the heart of any 360° Storyweaving Campaign. The other phases exist to support and drive audiences to the story components and will be discussed in this book, but will mainly be detailed and studied in future publications.

With creative fragmentation in the entertainment industry being one of the major obstacles to commercial transmedia design, we feel that when you can assemble a team of creative professionals from different industries and different backgrounds to work together from the inception of a project, the final product will be infinitely richer, deeper, and more coordinated.

So what is 360° Storyweaving?

Simply put, 360° Storyweaving is a specific type of transmedia. You may or may not have heard of the term *transmedia*. Chances are you haven't. And even if you have, you've probably heard it used incorrectly or have some unfortunate misconceptions of what it actually is.

For example, some folks think transmedia is simply equated with technology and new media, with the phrase, "Hey, I got an app for my book — transmedia, baby!" possibly being one of the most often used phrases of late. Others think transmedia strictly means extreme levels of fan interaction and participation. Some contend that transmedia is simply a marketing tool. and there are some who staunchly believe transmedia is forever tied to Alternate Reality Gaming. While technology, interaction, marketing, and ARGs definitely have roles in designing the 360° experience transmedia producers seek, at its core, transmedia is much simpler.

Essentially, transmedia is a fancy (and potentially scary) word that simply describes an innovative way to grow and expand a story. Again, while many content creators will use a tremendous variety of bells and whistles to make their transmedia experiences unique and tailored to their audiences, the basic principle of *story expansion* is the common denominator that ties all the approaches together.

Most transmedia professionals focus mainly on perfecting and innovating the end-user experience and become specialists in that regard. While this specialization is needed and really a very cool job to have, we believe content creators shouldn't skip to the experience part until they've perfected the art of expanding their story in the proper way.

Accordingly, in this book we're actually going to deal with what we call 360° Storyweaving — our own very specific and unique approach to taking a single story idea and growing and expanding it into an ever-increasing creative sandbox where the whole story transforms into a project greater than the sum of its parts.

Basically, it shows you how to make 1 + 1 = 3 instead of boring old 2. I always describe a great 360° Storyweaving project as a photo mosaic. Each picture in the mosaic has its own independent value and contribution. However, the magic happens when you step back and see it's not just a bunch of independent photos tossed together — there's a bigger, more rewarding picture to be seen. Of course, this takes planning and coordination, but if you can pull it off, you'll have crafted something not many people can create.

Again, 1 + 1 = 3. The old answer, my friends, is 2. In the twenty-first century, 2 is for the birds.

You can still be you.

I can hear you now:

"I'm a screenwriter/novelist/producer/poet! I don't want to change careers and become a transmedia professional!"

To be honest, I didn't actually hear you (if I could hear you right now, it'd be really creepy), but I've gotten that comment enough that I've become adept at anticipating it. All I can say is, "Don't fret." 360° Storyweaving is just a tool that will help you boil yourself back down to the essence of being a *storyteller*. Once there, you'll learn techniques that will help you when you turn your focus back to your area of creative expertise.

However, before I get ahead of myself (which I'm relatively sure I already have), let's go through a general, basic transmedia primer to make sure we're on the same page.

First of all, because it's such an emerging market, there isn't a consensus as to the "true" definition of transmedia. However, the

Producers Guild of America recently ratified an established credit for a Transmedia Producer. In its code of credits, the PGA simply defines Transmedia Narrative as at least three narrative storylines that all exist in the same fictional universe on a combination of platforms, including film, television, comics, mobile technology, short films, publishing, etc. The credit goes on to reinforce that the narratives aren't the same stories repurposed for different mediums. Instead they have to all be unique narratives.

Additionally, the credit defines a Transmedia Producer as someone who, among other things, oversees and is responsible for the creation, planning, development, and production and maintenance of the Transmedia Narrative across multiple platforms.

(For the entire text of the Transmedia Producer credit, visit the PGA's website, *www.producersguild.org*).

Others have defined transmedia as a collection of narrative components transmitted via numerous media and communication platforms which, when woven together by the audience, results in a richer and deeper story than any of its individual components.

Henry Jenkins, an American media scholar, USC professor, and trusty transmedia expert, has defined transmedia as:

"A process where integral elements of a fiction get dispersed systematically across multiple delivery channels for the purpose of creating a unified and coordinated entertainment experience. Ideally, each medium makes its own unique contribution to the unfolding of the story."

I tend to believe that all three of these definitions coexist politely and harmoniously in the same denotative space and are the definitions I apply to my own work.

Regardless of your perspective, however, a very broad take on the subject would describe transmedia as storytelling across multiple forms of media with each element making distinctive contributions to an audience's understanding of the storyworld. It's a powerful and profitable storytelling method that has developed out of extreme cultural shifts, which have made traditional storytelling methods outdated and ineffective with today's YouTube-driven Generation Z.

So, for example, a multimedia approach would tell a story in a film and then retell the same story in a book novelization and then retell the same story yet again in a comic book. The *Twilight* novels tell the same story as the films, which tell the same story as the graphic novels, etc. As you can see, a traditional multimedia approach is almost wholly built upon derivative works.

Conversely, a transmedia approach would develop a franchise universe not based on a character or a specific plot, but rather a complex fictional world that can sustain multiple interrelated characters and their subsequent stories. Once the universe is established, multiple stories are developed for a variety of mediums with key bits of information conveyed through the mediums.

Each one of these mediums tells unique stories that exist within the framework of the franchise universe and also give audience members unique perspectives and information. With this *additive comprehension* approach, there is no single source for gaining all the information needed to comprehend the universe.

For example, *The Matrix* isn't just a story about Neo and Morpheus. *The Matrix* is a story about a future where machines take over the planet and use humans as batteries. Part of that story is told through Neo's story via the film trilogy, part is told through the *Animatrix* animated feature, and part is told through the video games, and so on. The stories are all different, but still work together to form a great whole.

WHAT'S THE DIFFERENCE?

Because there hasn't been a consensus on the definition of "true" transmedia and because our process is unique, we thought we needed to avoid confusion and come up with our term. Hence, 360° Storyweaving.

360° speaks to broadening a story beyond the four corners of a page or the four corners of a screen and expanding into multiple mediums to a point where no matter where audiences turn, the story is there. Story speaks to, well, stories. Weaving communicates the level of coordination, cohesion, and connection you need to optimize the entire campaign.

The way people are consuming media has changed (and it's still changing) and 360° Storyweaving is an extension of that. Today's young people, the so-called "digital natives," are growing up in a connected world with technology that seems completely natural to them. They and others are changing and rewriting the rule book of what is possible. With people such as *Heroes* creator Tim Kring decreeing that one-channel storytelling is now considered archaic, the age of this new form of storytelling has only just begun.

WHY I DECIDED
TO WRITE
THE BOOK

I'M A PROCESS GUY.

I like to know what I'm doing and why I'm doing it, and I'm taking it upon myself to presume that I'm not alone.

Much to the frustration and discontent of people around me, I've always questioned things. It's not because I like to buck the proverbial system or that I get some bizarre satisfaction out of hassling people, but rather because I like to discover workflows and then burrow my way to the root to see how they were birthed and why they were developed.

Basketball scouts routinely refer to players who have "high basketball IQs," athletes who not only know they have to run off a screen and then make a backdoor cut, but also understand why they're doing it. Accordingly, I like to have a "high [*input any sort of workflow/process here*] IQ."

Likewise, when I encounter a situation where there's no discernible process or workflow, I immediately start implementing one. Maybe it's my board-game design background taking over or my analytical law school training kicking in or possibly an innate desire to control everything. Whatever the reason, chaos frustrates me. I have to know how and why, or else I get shifty and weird and it's safe to say that no one likes a guy who's shifty and weird.

This is why I love listening to Martin Scorsese talk about filmmaking. He breaks down storytelling to a science and can expose all the gears, belts, and wheels that make movies tick. He can take them apart, tell you the "how" and "why" and then put them together again all over the course of a good cup of coffee. When I began seeing films in the same way and then when I started viewing all stories as intricately designed machines, I was ruined forever. It was like in *The Matrix* when Neo first saw the matrix as all the 0s and 1s; I saw the process, I saw the science — and I fell in love.

So, when I first heard folks like Jeff Gomez and Henry Jenkins spreading (pun intended) the good word about this wonderful concept called transmedia, I was excited. As a storyteller, I was immediately drawn to the prospect of applying this storytelling science on a greater narrative scale, and its relevance to today's culture. Accordingly, I had our team spend the next year devouring every article, podcast, webinar, and conference devoted to transmedia.

I got the philosophy. I loved the theoretics surrounding it. I was challenged by the high-level intellectualism that came with its application and I was drawn to the narrative possibilities it presented. I was a sponge, soaking up terms like *spreadability*, *hyperdiegesis*, and *intertextuality*. Then one day I woke up and discovered no one had to convince me it was the way to go anymore. I was sold. What started then was an insatiable desire to know how to do it.

So, being a process guy, I started searching for a solid transmedia process, any process actually, but what I initially found were just other creative professionals debating definitions and staying on the theoretical side of transmedia. Remember in *Harry Potter and the Order of the Phoenix* when Dolores Umbridge refused to move beyond theory and Harry asked, "And how is theory supposed to prepare us for what's out there?" Well, Harry, I certainly could relate.

Don't get me wrong, theory is great. It's what got me hooked to begin with. It's the milk that I used to grow from a transmedia infant to a transmedia adult who was ready to leave home for the first time; however, at that point, milk wasn't what I needed. I was hungry. I needed food. I needed process.

Look, I'm sure there were processes out there, but I couldn't find them. I chalk it up to either me not looking hard enough, people not wanting to give away their workflows so as to maintain competitive advantage, or the information simply not being published yet because everything was so new. I would find "how" scraps scattered about — an article about how to construct a story bible, a workshop on how to develop a storyworld, a podcast about building engagement with your audience — but even when I would then burrow to the root of those bits and pieces, I wouldn't make satisfying "why" discoveries.

Transmedia was (and is still) in an exploration phase where most transmedia professionals and enthusiasts were seeking the same answers, so I completely understood why I was coming up short, though this didn't make it any less frustrating. Most importantly, though, I couldn't find a process that was tailored to fit exactly what we wanted One 3 Productions to do.

Basically, I needed a soup-to-nuts process that was replicable, teachable, fit what we did, guided us through the intimidation of the blank page, and actually facilitated the generation of transmedia-viable ideas and outputs.

So, we made one.

That, my friends, leads us to the primary goal of this book: to help usher transmedia out of the theoretical space and into a world of best practices by designing a great "how" and "why."

Let me take time to say that we're certainly not contending that our process is the best practice for the entire transmedia community. That would be a jerk thing to say. Likewise, I'm not trying to establish the objective definition of transmedia.

I assuredly don't think we've developed a magic bullet, nor do I think that universalist approach can be applied to any creative industry. I do feel, however, that our process can fit nicely into a best practices cupboard along with a nice collection of other best practices from other highly talented, creative, and intelligent folks.

I HATE THE BLANK PAGE. IT'S MY ENEMY.

As writers, it's our mission to defeat the blank page by filling it with a story; however, before most writers begin a project, it just sits there, staring at them and taunting them. So, what do they do?

They procrastinate. Once they start writing, it's nearly impossible to stop, but before the first words hit the page, they procrastinate as long as humanly possible.

Maybe I'm the only one who thinks this way, but I'd bet dollars to doughnuts there's a host of content creators who consider the blank page a shapeless and disorienting bully with no borders. I've found, though, that if I have a map to guide me through the Great White Wasteland, I can start the process with confidence and the blank page becomes much less intimidating. I know where the first step is leading me and I know the direction in which I'm headed.

Therefore, the second goal of this book is to help writers and content creators disarm the blank page by giving them a starting point, an end point, and every major checkpoint in between.

Before the Great Westward Expansion, embarking on a cross-country journey was intimidating and dangerous. Today, it's not. Why? Because it's been mapped for us. If I'm taking a road trip, I don't simply step out of my house in Los Angeles, get in the car and drive. I know I'm heading to Cincinnati and that I'll be stopping at the Grand Canyon, Santa Fe, Omaha, and St. Louis on the way. I have tremendous freedom in between those checkpoints, but at least I start the trip with a roadmap in my mind that allows me to budget, prepare, and maybe most importantly, convince others to join me.

STAR WARS IS OUR LOW BAR.

Again, the main reason we began developing our own process was that we needed something tailored to exactly what we wanted to do creatively and how we were thinking about our projects, and let me warn you now — we're big thinkers. Really big actually. To the point where most people think we're crazy. This, to us, means we're on the right track. It also means that any process we use needs to be scalable to fit our big, crazy vision.

I grew up a devoted fan of the *Star Wars* saga. I watched the films, owned the toys, donned the Underroos, played the role-playing game (Second Edition, not the original), and read the expanded-universe novels. Today, I marvel at the fact that George Lucas is still making so much money on one idea over thirty years after inception. Not only is there new content being produced in nearly every medium, there are dozens upon dozens of documentaries produced and books written that analyze every aspect of the franchise. It's astounding how this creative project has not only endured, but has continued to thrive over multiple decades. Lucas has accomplished this by imbedding his idea into not only the entertainment, publishing, and toy industries, but the culture as a whole.

With the *Harry Potter* series, I believe J. K. Rowling has created a similarly enduring work. I'm not just talking about book sales or box-office results. I'm not just talking about how J. K. Rowling is worth a billion dollars because of the franchise. I'm also referring to the massive multi-demographical, worldwide community she's built. The notion that a children's book about a young boy attending a school of wizardry, which was written on an old manual typewriter in Great Britain, now causes adults across the world to argue about what House the Sorting Hat would select for them, is amazing to me. Seriously, to make people that passionate about a piece of fiction is equally rare and awesome. Whether you're a fan of the series is beside the point. The cultural impact it's had is unquestionably remarkable.

Before some slick transmedia aficionado fires off an angry tweet about these two franchises not being "true transmedia," let me cut them off. I recognize that *Star Wars* isn't the best transmedia example because of the lack of additive comprehension in the different pieces. I also recognize that *Harry Potter* has existed as a straight adaptation before the announcement of *Pottermore*. So, when I fondly mention these projects, I'm focusing on their overall success and cultural impact rather than whether they fit snugly into a transmedia definition. If we can take the good things about these franchises and add those to our immersive transmedia experience we've designed from the ground up — watch out.

Are the accomplishments of Lucas, Rowling, and writers like Tolkien and C. S. Lewis exclusive to them? They created endurable works that have impacted people's lives in ways that 99.9% of other creative works haven't, but are they unique in their ability to create works of this nature? Absolutely not.

If George Lucas did it and J. K. Rowling did it, then so can we. And so can you. If you have the proper inspiration, a great idea, and you're armed with the right tools, I say chase the giant whale and don't settle for Nemo. Nemo is cool and all, but Nemo isn't for us (Nemo as in the size of the fish, not the $867 million *Finding Nemo* made at the box office — we would find a way to live with that).

Bottom line: We're going big. We're going for *Star Wars*-sized projects. We want to make J. K. Rowling jealous. We're going for works that are legacy-compliant. If my great-great-grandchildren aren't seeing one of our ideas thriving in their time, then we didn't think big enough.

However, I'm not just saying to dream that big in a "wouldn't that be cool" way. I'm telling you to *plan* that big from the inception of your project. If Lucas can get the results he's achieved when he didn't initially expect *Star Wars* to be more than a single film and had to expand the universe on the fly, how much more can we, as informed transmedia content creators, achieve when we think big and plan accordingly from the gate?

I'm telling you to go ahead and build a 90,000 square-foot house even though you may only use four rooms at first. It's much easier to do that than to keep adding on additions to a two-room starter home. Don't believe me? Dig up some interviews with Damon Lindelof and listen to him talk about how difficult it was to keep expanding *Lost* on the fly when the mysterious island was only designed for the pilot episode.

I know it seems like a lot to take on. You know why it seems like that? Because it's a lot to take on. But you can't expect to create a transmedia project that's as big as *Star Wars*, as good as *Lawrence of*

Arabia, sells as well as *Harry Potter* and lasts as long as the *Odyssey* without putting in some good old-fashioned sweat equity.

So, how do you plan for something that big? You follow our 360° Storyweaving process.

HERE'S WHERE WE'RE HEADED.

Okay, fair warning.

This book isn't for the faint of heart. It's a massive amount of information and, honestly, you will sometimes feel like you're trying to drink out of a fire hose. It'll tax your brain and rattle every single one of your creative habits to the core.

I think I've done a fair job in presenting it in a digestible format, but as with most things that are good for us, the 360° Storyweaving process admittedly is challenging. So, if you're up for the challenge, go ahead, settle in, and allow me to show you how to take a single concept or story and expand it into a massive creative architecture that will continue to grow.

The process we'll be going over consists of the following:
1. Laying a thematic foundation;
2. Creating a viable setting;
3. Developing a structured macro-story;
4. Developing self-contained micro-stories;
5. Making dynamic connections;
6. Deciding on multiple mediums; *and*
7. Exploring your stories vertically.

Throughout the book, primarily at the end of each chapter, are homework assignments. While these aren't necessarily required, I'd encourage you to take the time not to just read them, but to actually do them. Doing this will help drag transmedia out of the theoretical quicksand of your mind even faster and, by the end of the book, you'll actually have a very strong project framework to begin pursuing.

Also, throughout the book, I'll be referencing two of our own projects we currently have in development — *City of Refuge* and

Fury. We've obviously been using this 360° Storyweaving process on both projects and I think it will help you to see how we've been applying it.

Let's go over some terms.

Even if you're familiar with transmedia, I'm going to use some terms in this book that you'll almost certainly be unfamiliar with, have a slight chance of confusing you, and a 1.5% chance of frustrating you to the point of throwing this book across the room.

The terms work for our team, which is why I decided not to change them for the book, but as fair warning I'm going to generally go over some of them in an attempt to head off any possible confusion or frustration.

Or book throwing.

1. *Macro-Narrative*: The macro-narrative is the combination of every single one of your story elements, including everything listed below.

2. *Macro-Story*: This is the overarching storyline of your fictional universe. For now, think of it as your storyworld's historical timeline.

3. *Micro-Story*: This is a single plot and story that takes place within your macro-story.

4. *Nano-Stories*: This is a series of smaller stories that take place within your macro-story.

5. *Vertical Exploration*: These are miniature narrative bites that take place within either a micro-story or a nano-story that are normally edited out for space and time.

Think of these terms like the Russian matryoshka dolls that fit inside each other. The macro-narrative is the biggest doll, then the macro-story, then the micro-stories, and so on.

Trust me, don't try to understand them now. I simply wanted to allow them to marinate on your brain for a while so when we dig deep into them, you'll be ahead of the game.

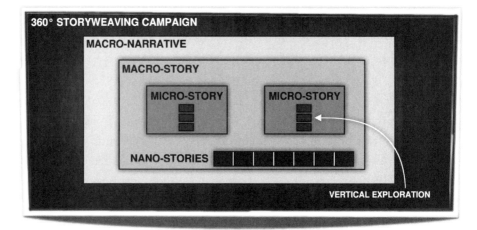

THE HONEST TRUTH.

Here's the thing — there is no recipe to an Oscar-winning film, a Grammy-winning song, or a best-selling novel. If I could crack that code, I would be a zillionaire, probably win a Nobel prize, and have enough power to somehow avoid LA traffic. So, if you're expecting to find a magic formula for success, you'll be disappointed. Some ideas hit and some ideas don't. Some folks execute and others drop the ball.

At the end of the day, you may or may not consider this to be true transmedia, depending on the definition to which you subscribe. Frankly, at One 3 Productions, we don't care about definitions as much as we care about creating projects that we think are cool, that we, as fans, would love to see in the marketplace, and that will ultimately connect our stories with the most people.

Regardless, I'm confident our 360° Storyweaving process will give you a better chance of long-term success, give your project some durability, and give you, the content creator, a structure that will help guide you through it all.

Honestly, at the end of the day, it comes down to the fact that it's helped us tremendously. It's guided us, it's challenged us, and has propelled our projects in creative directions we didn't previously think were possible. What this means is that there's a good chance it will help you, too.

So, we thought we'd share.

Enjoy.

HERE'S A QUICK SUMMARY.

The goals of this book are threefold:

- Move away from the theoretical side of transmedia and present one of the many possible "best practice" processes designed for practical application;

- Give writers and content creators a roadmap to use when they are facing a new project; *and*

- Present a scalable infrastructure that allows writers and content creators to develop their ideas and projects into endurable works that can be experienced and enjoyed for generations.

Imagine people 100 years in the future discovering your work, project, or idea for the first time. How will they view you? Is that how you want to be remembered? Preface your new idea with, "Dear Future Generation," and then think about how it will positively or negatively impact your personal legacy.

CHAPTER ONE

GET ON YOUR SOAPBOX!

SOAPBOX, VIABLE SETTING, MACRO-STORY, MICRO-STORIES, MULTIPLE MEDIUMS, DYNAMIC CONNECTIONS, VERTICAL EXPLORATION

WHERE DO WE START?

As with most projects, knowing where to begin is one of, if not the, most important steps to execute properly. If you don't, you'll only experience grief later in the process because you set off in a wrong direction and are forced to backtrack and revise. Listen, there's so much to do, why not just get it right the first time?

So, the first thing you need to do is build your **soapbox**. Figuratively speaking, of course. Unless, you actually need a soapbox, which in that case, happy building.

In the nineteenth century, people would plop down actual soapboxes so they could be elevated for a public speech. Generally, these speeches had to do with politics, but at the heart of it, the speeches were opinionated, passionate, agenda-driven, and rabble-rousing. People who used soapboxes were, predictably, called "soapboxers." That's the first step — using your project as a soapbox and proudly accepting the label of a modern-day soapboxer.

You may call it *theme*, moral premise, message, agenda, or even meta-story, but whatever you call it, it's going to become the foundation of your project.

WHY START WITH THEME?

Why not start by designing characters, strategizing what mediums to use, or creating a setting or fleshing out your supercool original idea you sketched out last year but haven't done anything with? It's because theme gives your creative decisions purpose and allows your project to connect with your audience on a greater level.

I'm not saying your story can't be good without a strong message. I'm saying that stories without strong thematic foundations are like sugar rushes — they get you excited for a bit, but can't sustain you for a long period of time because they don't have substance. Conversely, stories set on strong thematic soapboxes are more likely to endure and continue to resonate because even though the culture may change, universal themes tend to remain intact and continually connect with people across multiple generations.

Have you ever watched an old movie and found it difficult to relate to because the actors talk differently than you talk, they act differently than you act, things look differently than they do now, and culture has significantly changed since the movie was released? Well, if the movie has a strong thematic foundation, that's what will connect with you, allow you to look past all the surrounding irrelevance and keep you watching.

Honestly, the thematic heartbeat of *It's a Wonderful Life* is the only reason I would still watch that film. I know Jimmy Stewart is good and all, but there are so many things that just don't click with me. But, I'll still check it out because despite the fact it was made before my parents were even born, it carries a great message — that everyone's life has meaning.

The coolness of plots fades over time, the initial ability of characters to relate will wane, and the wittiest line of dialogue in 2013 may be glazed over thirty years from now without even being noticed. But your theme, your message, those things you want to say to the world, your soapbox — they hold up through the years.

Why should anyone care?

Seriously. Why should anyone care about your project?

Why should anyone give you money that they've spent hours of their lives earning? Because they'll be entertained? In a recessive economy and a ridiculously saturated entertainment landscape, simply being able to entertain for a few hours isn't a safe bet.

Don't get me wrong, I'm not saying entertainment is bad. It's absolutely essential. I'm merely advocating that you inspire *and* entertain because a strong soapbox and an entertaining story aren't mutually exclusive ideals.

You'll build a bigger audience.

Simon Sinek gave a TED Talk where he presented a concept he calls the *Golden Circle* and spoke on the reason you should always start with "why."

By the way, as a side note, if you don't check out TED Talks on a regular basis then you should because they're awesome videos that give tremendous insights into people on the forefront of innovation, creativity, and leadership.

In the TED Talk (and also in his book *Start with Why*) he explores how great leaders, whether they be politicians, creative visionaries, filmmakers, inventors, or corporate CEOs, not only motivate people to act, but also inspire people to follow them.

He points out that all industries, creative and otherwise, needs to motivate people to act in order to sustain themselves. Painters need to motivate people to buy their paintings. Writers need to motivate readers to buy their books. Marketers need to motivate people to actually act on their calls-to-action. Filmmakers need to motivate audiences to watch their movies. Restaurant owners need to motivate people to eat at their establishments.

But how do you motivate people?

When it comes to motivations, people tend to be swayed by incentives — price, convenience, social benefit, etc. However, when you can *inspire* people to act, as opposed to just motivating them, you actually impart an innate sense of purpose and belonging, which is so much more valuable. As a result, you don't just start building an audience or a fan base, you also start cultivating a devoted following.

Motivated consumers, because they are responding to external incentives, will almost always fall away when those disincentives appear — the cost is too high, the theater is too far away, none of their friends are into it, etc. It's not worth it to them because their connection is a superficial one. Devoted followers, however, are willing to pay more if needed, endure inconvenience if required, and even suffer a bit if they're called to do so.

Why?

They're following you not because you have the coolest project around, but because you believe what they believe and that always has value. You may think I'm getting too deep, but when what you create starts to only serve as proof as to what you believe, you'll start connecting to your audience in ways you've never planned.

The diagram below actually shows how inspirational leaders communicate and operate. It documents a pattern of thought and action that any content creator, with a little discipline, can put to use.

This shows the order in which people communicate ideas in an attempt to get others to do something they wouldn't do on their own accord.

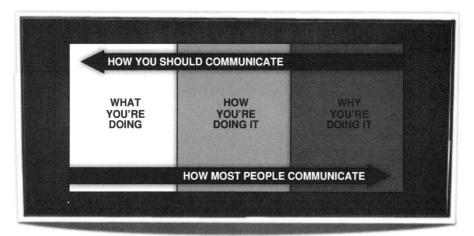

In the creative space, when trying to motivate audience members, financiers, or people they want to acquire the property, writers, producers, and creators typically work from the outside in. They know what their product is, so that's where they begin.

> *"I've written this amazing sci-fi script that is screaming to be shot in 3D!"*

If they actually move past the "what," they'll start describing the "how" of their project.

> *"I saw how successful* Avatar *was, so I really used that as a template for how to maximize action, story, and visuals."*

Now at this point, most everyone stops. My thinking is most people don't ever consider "why," so they honestly wouldn't know what to say, or if they have, they don't think the person they're pitching to actually cares.

Truly inspirational leaders and artists work from the inside out. They start with the "why" of their project, go to the "how" and eventually finish with the "what."

> *"I really wanted to communicate to young people how destructive it is to be driven by pain and anger and, no matter what kind of tragedy they've dealt with, the best thing to do is to let it go and move on.*
>
> *So I ended up using a great combination of visuals, action, and story that I knew young people would respond to, especially after seeing how* Avatar *broke so many box office records.*
>
> *What I have now is an amazing sci-fi script that's screaming to be shot in 3D!"*

This just feels different. It has more substance and I promise you, it will ultimately yield you better results.

Let's say you're having this conversation with a producer you want to attach to your project. If he likes science fiction movies, he may be motivated to read your script even if you start with "what." That is, of course, if he has time (which always works to de-motivate people), if he's even looking for a new project, if he doesn't already have 403 other sci-fi scripts on his desk, if he doesn't think you're a hack because you don't have any IMDB credits, and if he doesn't think you'll sue him because you've brought this up unsolicited.

As you can imagine, working your way through these objections is difficult when you're only armed with a "what." But, if you connect with him on the "why," it's more likely these other factors won't matter as much and he'll read your script. Why? Because, there's a good chance he believes the same thing and, ultimately, people don't buy what you do as much as why you're doing it.

Apple doesn't market themselves as a company that makes beautiful, easy-to-use computers (their "what"), or that hires the best designers and most brilliant minds in the marketplace (their "how"). They start with how they want to make everyone's lives easier and how they don't believe people should have to settle for the status quo when it comes to technology (their "why"). This causes them to go out and hire the best designers and the most brilliant minds in the industry (their "how") and, in the end, they produce beautiful, easy-to-use computers.

Rev. Dr. Martin Luther King, Jr. didn't motivate people to go to Washington, D.C., on a sweltering August day by laying out a logical twelve-point plan on how to fix the country's racial divide. Instead, he inspired people by telling them what he believed, conveying his dreams, and explaining why change was necessary. He found people who believed what he believed and he built a following.

In Hollywood, a huge part of the filmmaking game is getting people (agents, producers, actors, janitors, the guy on Craigslist you bought the used futon from, etc.) to read your scripts. If you can get anyone to actually read anything, it's a huge victory and worthy accomplishment. That's the same game everyone is playing, which means the producers and the agents don't have to take all of them — they have their pick of the litter. However, as a company, we at One 3 Productions purposely avoid asking anyone to read our stuff.

Seriously.

Because we're a mission-driven company, whenever we meet with industry contacts, we always start with why we're doing what we're doing. From there, we talk about how we use a transmedia approach to develop the projects and eventually get to what our project actually is about. Every single time we've done that, the person we're meeting with, be it a studio executive or an actor, has asked *us* if he or she could read *our* script. No joke. It's because they see our substance, our long-term value, our passion, and our purpose and those factors immediately disarm all the objections, legitimate or otherwise, they have cocked and ready to use against us.

When you start with why you're doing what you're doing, you're connecting to people's souls rather than dueling with their logic.

Now apply this to your transmedia project.

Too many times I have heard transmedia producers begin talking about their projects by telling me about their tech, their apps, and their whiz-bang platforms. Almost every time, I tune out. Talented folk that have awesome razzle-dazzle technology with their projects are a dime a dozen. Unless you've actually invented a new piece of technology, your platforms aren't what make your project unique, and even if you have, it doesn't mean I'm completely sold. I may be interested in your new toy, but why should I be interested in your story?

Instead, use the method I've been detailing. *Why* are you even creating this project? This is the soapbox/thematic foundation we've been talking about. *How* are you doing it? Well, if you're following our process, you're using a macro-narrative approach to transmedia. What are you creating? This would be your individual stories, components, and whiz-bang, razzle-dazzle tech elements that you love so much.

This will actually help you creatively.

Some creative professionals, from songwriters to authors to designers, refer to a destructive phenomenon called "scope creep." This is when the scope of a project starts to grow and grow and grow and grow and grow until the whole project becomes messy, unfocused, awkward, and ultimately fragile. If you, as the content creator, haven't created your project with a steely focus, how can you reasonably expect your audience to focus? In today's entertainment-saturated culture, if you lose someone's attention for five seconds, they're off playing *Angry Birds* and you have as much of a chance of regaining them as fans as they have of beating the game with the boring red birds. Not likely.

How do you combat scope creep? You form borders to your project. To make a sandbox, you don't start by dumping a bunch of sand on the ground. You begin by building the four walls that contain it. Likewise, puzzle masters never start a puzzle by trying to figure out the middle. Puzzle masters worth their salt start on the edges; they define their borders.

Your soapbox is what will form those borders for your project. It will define a very clear narrative space for you to sink your teeth

into and allow you to carve out a more focused project by informing every single creative decision you make. A thematic foundation
and border empower you to refuse anything that falls outside its
scope. If something doesn't reconcile with your theme, it's not allowed. If a creative decision starts to tear down your soapbox, you
ditch it.

Trust me. Adhering to a strong thematic soapbox will help you
from straying off the path. It's like when you go hiking and every
now and then you see a sign that says KEEP ON THE PATH.
Some may say those signs are infringing on your hiking freedom.
I say they're helping you not be eaten by a mountain lion and you
should thank the guy who put them there.

START AN ARGUMENT.

Remember in high school and college when you would have
to write persuasive essays? Building your soapbox and laying your
thematic foundation work the same way. Your theme will simply
be an assertion (or assertions) you want to make to the world. Your
entire project and every story you write will be your argument as to
why your assertion is true.

The Lord of Rings series is actually centered on a number of
themes, one of which is that no matter how small you are, you can
still do something great. Throughout the books, Tolkien is con-
stantly making that argument. Every time the Hobbits unexpectedly succeed at doing something great, his assertion is strength-
ened, and by the end, he proves his assertion true.

In the Craig Brewer film, *Hustle & Flow*, the theme that reso-
nates above all others is that no matter how far off the path you've
gone, you should always pursue your dreams. Every crazy situation
Djay finds himself in deals with that question and is Brewer's argument as to why that assertion is, in fact, true. When the film is over,
you end up not only agreeing with Brewer concerning his thematic
assertion, but you also find yourself saying, "Hey, if a pimp in the
ghettos of Memphis can change his life and achieve his dreams
then so can I."

Good storytellers, though, put pressure on their thematic assertions and take you through a thematic roller coaster before ultimately proving their assertions true. So, when you watch *Hustle & Flow*, you find yourself going through a very dynamic "will he/won't he" process. You think he can change, then you think he won't, then you think he can, then you think he won't, and so on.

Finally, when Djay beats the tar out of Skinny Black in a bathroom stall, you completely write him off as a potential candidate for change. But, in the end, Djay pulls it together and you see the fulfillment of the theme in the character's life.

Brewer obviously and purposely crafted the story this way. First and foremost, it's to make the story more dramatic, tense, and interesting for the audience. But also, on a thematic level, you need your argument to be seen as realistic and credible, so you want to put pressure on the theme in every way possible.

How do you choose?

It's easy.

Just find something you're passionate about. Identify a cause that makes you cry. Pick something that gets you out of bed in the morning and that you find yourself talking about to other people. What are the topics that cause you to raise your voice or to wave your arms around like a crazy person? What do you want your kids to learn? What do you want to teach future generations? Your project is your soapbox, so now that you have a stage, what do you want to say? What do you believe? Or what don't you believe?

Be careful not to just pick open-ended topics, though. I just googled "most common literary themes" and I pulled up this list:

1. Good versus evil;
2. Man versus nature;
3. Love and friendship;
4. Man versus society;
5. Man versus himself;
6. Fate versus freewill; *and*
7. Suffering versus redemption.

This is not what I'm referring to when I'm talking about your theme, message, or soapbox. These can, however, help you find your soapbox, but these are just categories. Remember that your soapbox should be opinionated and passionate. It's the difference between a regular newspaper article (just the facts, expository, etc.) and an editorial opinion piece.

Sure, *Star Wars* dealt with good versus evil, but Lucas didn't just present the battle and back away — he actually *said* something about it. He didn't just present the struggle between suffering and redemption, he openly declared that even one of the most evil dudes in the galaxy can be redeemed. That's a bold statement, but he wasn't afraid to say it.

Be opinionated. Have a voice and a unique perspective. It's the difference between saying, "Racism is my theme," and saying, "My theme is that racism is evil." The latter is much stronger and will elicit more of a response from an audience.

If someone walks up to you and says, "Love and friendship," you'll probably just look at her weird. But, if the same person walks up to you and says, "I think a man who is loved and who has friends is the richest man in the world," you'll have a completely different reaction — a better reaction. Plus there's now room for dialogue and interaction whereas before there wasn't.

That being said, choosing an open-ended topic isn't a bad place to start per se. Just don't stop there. But if you can't think of a theme right off the bat, just choose a topic. Once you have the topic, write an opinion on that topic.

For example, we'll take the innocuous open-ended topic of "education." That was easy enough to select. Now, just write an opinion about that topic.

Education is good.

Okay, let's make it stronger by punching it up.

Everyone should be educated.

We're getting there. Let's punch it up again.

Everyone should be educated, but education can come in many forms.

Now you're saying something. Can we make it any stronger? *Everyone should be educated, but the public school system isn't the only path to education — life experience is the greatest teacher around.*

Wow. Now that's a good opinion. Will everyone agree? No, but your project is your way to convince them.

In our *City of Refuge* transmedia project, our soapbox is simple and twofold:

1. No one is too bad for redemption; *and*

2. It's love and goodness that will cause people to truly change, rather than fear, punishment, and judgment.

In our *Fury* transmedia project, our soapbox is that if you're burdened by fear, guilt and pain and let them drive your actions, they'll ultimately destroy you.

They're not complicated. They're not really controversial. But, at the same time, they're very pointed, opinionated assertions and they're truths that we know can help people. Throughout the creative process, they informed everything we did and every decision we made.

I took it upon myself to pull some examples of thematic foundations from my collection of books, games, and films. Note how focused and opinionated they are and how they're not just exploring vague, open-ended topics.

Love is the most powerful force in the universe.

The love of money will always lead people to do evil things.

Fear is a very real, destructive, spiritual force.

Lying always has consequences.

You shouldn't take your life for granted.

Revenge will never make you whole.

Angels are real and are active in our lives.

Women should have the same opportunities as men in the marketplace.

Death should be viewed as a promotion rather than a tragedy.

Kids shouldn't be too eager to grow up.

Humans shouldn't try to play God.

Conformity is a type of bondage.

Society will always need a hero and a savior.

Life is too short to waste at a job you hate.

Childbirth is something every woman should experience at least once.

Childbirth isn't necessarily for every woman.

No matter how old you are, you should pursue your dreams.

All men are dogs.

Crime doesn't pay.

No matter what nationality, race, or gender, we're all the same inside.

The bond between father and son is more special than any other bond that exists.

Marriage is the cornerstone of society.

We shouldn't be so attached to material items.

You are the architect of your own life.

Character is the true measure of a person.

American ideals are still worth defending.

Your personal happiness is not the most important thing in the world.

Wisdom should be sought before anything in life.

Evil must be confronted and defeated.

Leaders lead by example.

A life lived without love is a life half lived.

True capitalists are what make America great.

The American banking system is broken and needs to be replaced.

Idealism works, even in an imperfect world.

Everyone we encounter has an effect on us.

True friendship never gives up.

Honesty is the best policy.

Beauty is in the eye of the beholder.

You have to love yourself before you can begin to love others.

Everyone's voice is worth being heard.

Drugs are always bad.

Divorce is always destructive for a child.

Just because you've been divorced, doesn't mean you can't have a loving family.

Just because you're old, doesn't mean you have to give up on finding love.

There's a plan for everyone's life.

The spiritual world is just as real as the physical world in which we live.

Everything happens to us for a reason.

Debt is a type of slavery.

The environment is worth protecting.

Violence is never the answer.

The lesser of two evils is still evil.

If you stay eternally positive, you'll always be positioned for success.
You can sell without selling out.

Gossip can lead to your downfall.

Life is never as bad as you think.

The only people you can trust in life are your friends.

You're never too old to reinvent yourself.

INVESTMENTS WILL COME EASIER.

If you're creating in the independent arena, chances are you're looking for investment capital. Every single transmedia conference we attend, people are looking for money. Every single film festival we go to, people are looking for money. Every board game event we attend, people are looking for money. Independent artists need money for their projects and most of the time, it seems nearly impossible to find, outside of crowdfunding services like Kickstarter or Indiegogo.

If you're looking for large-scale equity investments, though, you have to find people who are liquid enough to invest a sizable amount of money. If you actually find someone like this, you have to convince him or her to take your meeting and then if you get a meeting, you have to convince him or her to actually invest. This can be an exhausting process, but it's not impossible. People do it everyday.

Go to the American Film Market sometime and you'll find hundreds of independent films that, honestly, are awful. Many are great, but most are horrible. But the fact that the producers are at AFM looking for distribution means the movies (I won't even call them films) got made, which means someone financed them. That should encourage you. People are still putting millions of dollars into bad movies, which stands to reason that if you have a good movie, you have a chance. While a 360° Storyweaving approach can't be a guarantee for successs, it will definitely *increase* your chance for success.

The first way to find more financing success will be, as we discussed previously, to pitch your project from the inside out. You'll discover that if you can find potential financiers who believe what you believe, you'll have many more conversations about your theme than you will about the dreaded ROI (Return on Investment). You'll still have conversations about ROI, but if you can connect with a financier's soul, he'll try much harder to figure out and rationalize the investment. Obviously, there's no guarantee, but at least by standing on your soapbox, you'll start off on better footing.

You'll fish in a bigger pond.

If you're like most independent artists, it's probably proving difficult to find potential investors in the first place. Let's be honest, the investor/investee ratio isn't in your favor. Don't fret, though, because using your soapbox properly will begin to change that dynamic.

By using the Internet and any other (preferably free) vehicle to get your vision and theme out, you'll start to connect with people who believe what you believe and begin to cultivate followers. That, by itself, will open you up to a whole new world of potential investors. People who you may have never targeted as potential investors or may have never considered themselves as potential investors will start to pop up because your theme will draw them out.

Under normal circumstances, there's no way middle-class Ms. Jones would touch her nest egg in order to fund your project. She's never made an investment into any creative project, she doesn't have an interest in pushing for innovation, and she has two kids she's putting through private school. Under our previous analysis, there's potential motivation for her to invest (a chance at a positive return on her investment); however, there are too many other disincentives for your project to overcome. No *bueno* for you.

However, when she finds herself moved by the message of your project, discovers that your theme is how she's felt for years, and deems your project a *cause* worthy of her support, she feels more compelled to get involved. The disincentives are still there, but she's more willing to fight through them because the purpose of the project has resonated with her on an emotional and possibly spiritual level.

When we began the process of securing investments for our *City of Refuge* project, we shot a short video where we talked about the theme and the purpose of the project. We published it on You-Tube and on our Facebook page and a few days later we were contacted by a couple who wanted to invest $10,000. We didn't seek them out or ask them to invest. In fact, they're not a couple we would have even thought of as potential investors. But our theme resonated with them and *they ended up contacting us*.

How cool is that?

IF YOU PITCH THIS WAY, CREATE THIS WAY.

If you talk about your project from the inside out and people respond accordingly, it only makes sense to create your transmedia project from the inside out as well. When your creative process begins with "why," it'll be much more natural to communicate and pitch the project from the inside out on the backend.

Plus, it will ensure that your theme and your message stay consistent throughout every story element and every creative decision.

IT'S NOT AS RISKY AS YOU THINK.

Again, everyone may not agree with the thematic argument you're trying to make, but that's fine. It's your job to convince them. Don't withdraw your voice just because you don't want to risk someone disagreeing. Don't fall into the trap of playing it safe by sticking to a story that simply has a cool plot spread across some whiz-bang, razzle-dazzle tech.

Safe is good for sidewalks and swimming pools, but life is short. You've been put on the earth and given a unique voice for a reason. Take advantage of that privilege, add it to your creativity, get out of your comfort zone, and go do something with some meaning.

Now, go build your soapbox.

HERE'S A QUICK SUMMARY.

The first step in the 360° Storyweaving creative process is to identify your thematic premise.

Doing this will help you focus your project while simultaneously informing all of your creative decisions.

Beginning with theme, both creatively and in the way you market the project, will not only motivate people to act, but will also inspire fellow believers and start something even better than a fan base — a following.

Pitching your project from the inside out will not only get more people to read your work, but it will also give you greater success finding investment capital.

Moreover, you'll find that there will be even more potential investors to approach because you've tapped into people who believe what you believe.

Your project's theme will act as an opinion, as opposed to the exploration of a general topic, with the body of the project acting as the argument proving its truth.

HERE'S YOUR HOMEWORK.

1. Write down ten topics you're passionate about. From that list pick the one or two you think the world and future generations need to learn about the most.

2. Now, write a strong opinion about the topic(s) in one or two sentences.

CHAPTER TWO

BUILD YOUR CHARACTERS A HOUSE TO LIVE IN

SOAPBOX, **VIABLE SETTING**, MACRO-STORY,
MICRO-STORIES, MULTIPLE MEDIUMS,
DYNAMIC CONNECTIONS, VERTICAL EXPLORATION

PUT ON YOUR PANTS BEFORE YOUR SHOES.

Now it's time to develop a setting for your project and I'm not talking about a simple backdrop for any old story where the setting is a generic city, or forest, or just outer space. The purpose of this chapter is to create a **viable setting** and not to let you create any setting you want. This means you need to create a living, breathing multidimensional narrative world that has depth, history, and the potential to facilitate multiple stories across multiple platforms for many years to come.

You may be wondering, though, why we don't first design awesome characters and then worry about where to stick them. I mean, don't great stories start with great characters? Fair questions that actually have a very simple answer.

Yes, great stories need great characters. Yes, you can't have a great story without them; however, right now we're not developing stories. We're designing a world where the stories will be *set*. We'll get to the story part, but not just yet, which means the characters can wait patiently as well. Don't get me wrong — I love coming up with characters as much as the next writer. But, at this point, this isn't a question of love, it's a question of order.

In this process, if you come up with a character first, it's like putting your shoes on before your pants. Have you ever tried that? It's difficult and ends up taking longer (if you can do it at all) and there's a distinct possibility that you'll fall over and hit your head on the dresser, so why even make the attempt? This isn't to say that pants are more important than shoes. This isn't anti-shoeism. Both are equally important to a snazzy look and a nice wardrobe. All I'm saying is there's an order to how you put them on.

Likewise, this isn't a "setting versus character" argument. It's an "awesome setting first, then awesome characters second" argument. Remember the *Reading Rainbow* theme song? After the first verse sells the benefits of reading, the second verse then starts with the line, "I can go *anywhere*." Then, the third verse begins with, "I can be *anything*." "Anywhere" speaks to setting and "anything" points to characters.

Awesome setting *then* awesome characters. LeVar Burton would agree.

Your characters will thank you.

Trust me when I say a great setting is the best thing you can do for your characters and their stories. Your characters will be more interesting because you've given them a sandbox to explore, your stories will have more depth because there will be more backstory to reveal, and you'll be able to give your concept "legs" a whole heck of a lot easier because there's more room to breathe.

You may think you don't need a sprawling setting because you already have a concept or story and both are small and indie, but this is about planning for the future. Remember when I said to go ahead and build the 90,000-square-foot house even though you'll only fill up a few rooms right now? Well, the setting is going to be that house, the rooms are the stories, and the people who live there will be the characters.

In *The Matrix*, the whole Neo/Morpheus story about being inside a computer program is really cool, but when the filmmakers set those characters, as well as the concept, inside a future where machines have taken over and use humans as energy sources, they then had room to explore beyond just Neo and Morpheus.

In the same vein, the most interesting thing about *Harry Potter,* ironically, isn't Harry — it's Hogwarts, the boarding school he and the rest of the children attend. Hogwarts does what any great setting does — it gives Harry context, it gives his actions meaning, and makes him more alive. Actually, it's not just the school (though the school is the anchor of the setting) but also the collective surroundings of the Forbidden Forest, the Black Lake, the surrounding greenhouses, the Quidditch pitch, and Diagon Alley.

Let's do an exercise so I can demonstrate the importance of a great setting.

Remove Hogwarts from *Harry Potter.* What happens? I'd wager you can hit very similar plot points and create similar situations and create the exact same arc for Harry even if you put him, Ron, Hermione, and the rest in a public school building in Riverside, CA. You can have very similar stories but they wouldn't be as timeless or as interesting.

Set the *Star Wars* saga in modern-day Europe. Palpatine is the dictator. Vader is his general. Luke is a farm boy from Italy. Princess Leia is the leader of an underground resistance. Could it be good? Sure, but it wouldn't be as magical and I'm not confident it would yield the mountain of features, novels, toys, comics, cartoons, audio dramas, video games, and board and roleplaying games that it has over the years.

Tolkien with *The Lord of the Rings*, James Cameron with *Avatar*, and C. S. Lewis with *The Chronicles of Narnia* all literally designed new worlds with an astonishing level of detail. Can you imagine *Avatar* without Pandora? Or Frodo without Middle-earth? Would Aslan still be the same taken out of Narnia and placed in a generic African setting? If you've read the *Fables* series by Bill Willingham, you would agree the existence of Fabletown adds a coolness to the story that wouldn't exist if the fairy tale characters were simply scattered around in different places.

Removing the settings from these tales would be fatal to the narrative. Now, leave the setting intact and try to remove a character.

We know what would happen to *The Lord of the Rings* if we tried to extract Middle-earth, but what if we didn't have Frodo? Well, Frodo is an awesome character, but it wouldn't be fatal because there are thousands of other stories to tell and characters to deal with. Likewise, we can't remove Pandora from *Avatar*, but I'm confident that despite their being great characters, a great story can be told on Pandora without Neytiri and Jake.

There's just something about taking great characters and great plots and surrounding them with a well-designed, interesting, and rich setting that is a recipe for creative longevity. A great setting elevates everything it touches by providing a deeper and larger canvas on which to paint. Characters become more dynamic, stories become deeper — everything is made better when the setting transcends the dull, static backdrop to which it so often relegated.

Um, too late.

You may already have a story written, a character designed, or even a film or graphic novel finished and you've never, ever considered your setting.

Are you toast? Not at all. Honestly, you may have already developed a great setting that'll work swimmingly. How can you find this out? Do an exercise like the ones we were just doing. See what happens when you remove your main character. Is what's left still interesting? Can you get more stories out of it from other characters or other perspectives? If so, rock on. You're off to a good start and you can use the rest of this chapter for strengthening and tweaking.

If not, then your main character is being forced to uphold the entire project and you'll need to go back and punch up your setting. Don't fret, though. You'll just have to do some backtracking, but you can still make it work.

If your work can be changed (if it's still in development, a script-level concept, or a written work that hasn't been published), it's as simple as taking all your characters and plots and going through the 360° Storyweaving process outlined in this book, obviously with your characters and plots in mind.

If you're absolutely in love with your characters and plots, use them as project borders along with your theme. Therefore, as you go through the setting design process, your pre-established ideas will inform you as to what will work in your setting and what won't. Even if your plots don't change, you should be able to quickly identify how your setting can be expanded around your plots and characters to become more vibrant and alive.

If you're not married to your plot ideas and characters and are open for more widespread change, it's even easier. Just start from the beginning of the 360° Storyweaving process with a general knowledge your characters and plots exist and use them as a general jumping-off point creatively. Once you're in the process, you'll find your characters, location, plots, and everything else you've come up with will begin to be reshaped and molded into something greater. Some things may have to be ditched altogether and, if so, just think of it like pruning a tree — ultimately it's for the best.

Our *City of Refuge* concept actually started with the idea of one character — a violent, big city ex-con who hides in a small, country town as the pastor of its colorful, quirky church. When we started going through the 360° Storyweaving Process, we sidelined the character, as well as the rough story we had written for him. When we extracted the character, what was left was a small, country town. We decided to use the town as the setting, although we knew we had to punch it up and make it more interesting for it to be a commercial concept. However, once we started that process (described in the next chapter), the concept for the character we developed shifted quite a bit and the story outline we developed for him had to be completely thrown out. But, because we knew where we were headed with the 360° Storyweaving Process, we knew that, ultimately, the character would be stronger and his stories would be better.

If, however, you've already shot a film or have already published your novel, you're in a slightly different boat, but, again, all is not lost. You simply go through this process, but instead of having your stories and characters change with the process, you'll just have to lock them in as canon and create around them. It's not ideal, but it's still doable and realistic.

We actually do quite a bit of consulting for filmmakers on how to take their completed films and transmediate them with our process. Like I said, it's a little trickier, but you'd be surprised at how far an imagination with a storyweaving mindset can get you.

We consulted on a story idea about a famous television marriage counselor who gets divorced and, after being publicly disgraced, is forced to move back to his hometown, live with his parents, and work at his family's pizza parlor. The creators didn't use our macro-narrative process, never considered setting, and were initially only interested in telling the story of this guy trying to get his life back on track. That left us with the task of going back in and defining the setting so we could find more narrative space to tell more stories moving forward.

When we extracted the main character, we were left with the small town setting, much like in the *City of Refuge* situation. However, unlike the *City of Refuge* project, we were unable to punch up this suburban setting and make it interesting. So, what else could we do? Well, after the character was extracted and the small town was scratched off the list of setting candidates, what was left was the family pizza parlor where this character was forced to work. We made the decision to have the crazy, quirky, family pizza parlor, that started to double as a counseling service via pizza delivery, be the setting of the universe and all other stories and components be set in and around it. When the creators developed the story, they didn't imagine the pizza parlor playing such an important part, which shows when you approach a story with a macro-narrative mindset, you'll end up exploring rabbit holes you never would have imagined from the outset.

Bottom line: with a 360° Storyweaving franchise, you need as many stories as you can get, and love it or hate it, the more stories you want, the bigger, more viable setting you need.

HYPER-DI-WHAT'S-IT?

Hyperdiegesis is the term used to describe the creation of a vast and detailed narrative space, only a fraction of which is ever directly seen or encountered within the text, but which nonetheless appears to operate according to principles of internal logic and extension. To use a cliché, it's like revealing only the tip of the iceberg.

Once you're finished with this chapter, feel free to consider yourself a Hyperdiegetic Architect. Put that on your LinkedIn profile and see how many of your friends you impress.

However, again, I'm a process guy, so just like there are three phases to our 360° Storyweaving franchises and seven distinct creative elements of a well-designed 360° Storyweaving franchise, there are eight elements you need to implement and consider when constructing your viable setting.

We'll be exploring each one of these elements in detail as we go through the rest of this chapter, as well as giving you homework throughout so you can continue to work on your project while wading your way through the book. The elements are:

1. People Group;
2. Location;
3. High Concept;
4. Broad Geographical Boundaries;
5. Special Sauce;
6. Unfamiliarity;
7. Setting History; *and*
8. Social Segments and Status Ladders

The first three elements make up the heart and guts of your setting with numbers four through eight serving as enhancements that will take it to the next level.

People Group.

As stated previously, when developing a viable setting for a transmedia project, you have to think broader than individual characters. Instead of individuals, the first step to a viable setting is to start brainstorming *people groups*. For example, rather than focusing on a math teacher character, focus on math teachers as a whole. Likewise, don't think about Harry or Ron or Hermione, but rather think in people groups and social labels such as wizards, students, or teenagers.

As an aside, I've always wanted to explore the world of street performers, particularly the ones who impersonate celebrities and fictional characters. I think that would be a fascinating people group to write about. I got the idea when I saw a street performer who was wearing a crude, handmade Spider-Man costume that probably took him days to stitch. I was intrigued by the mindset of someone who would spend days hand-stitching a costume just to stand on a sidewalk peddling for tips. However, to create a viable transmedia setting, I needed to step back from that one character and broaden my view to the entire people group — street performers. Said Spider-Man impersonator would simply be one character in a greater people group and simply one story in a greater universe.

Location.

Once you have your people group, you need to think of what kind of location will house them. Is it a town? Is it a world? Is it a building? Is it a galaxy? This is the second step in designing a viable transmedia setting.

In the *Harry Potter* series, the people groups are wizards, witches, students, teachers, etc., and the location is Hogwarts. Using my street performer example, the location could be Hollywood Boulevard. In our *City of Refuge* project, it's the small town of Always. *Batman* has Gotham City. *Lost* has an island.

Be sure to make your location as definable as possible, though. Instead of "the woods," focus it to Sherwood Forest. Instead of "the ocean," sharpen it to the bottom of the Marianas Trench. The more definable you make your setting, the more it will start to come alive.

The High Concept.

The *high concept* is the creative mechanism you're going to push your people group and location through to propel them from being just an idea to being a *commercially viable* idea.

Track with me, though, because I'm going to commit a shocking break in protocol and use some general story concepts simply to illustrate what a high concept actually is even though this chapter isn't about characters and their stories, but rather settings.

To put it as simply as possible, a high concept is a concept that is immediately interesting to someone; one that has obvious potential and can hook someone from the gate.

It seems simple enough, but I'm shocked at how many low concepts I see on the shelves at a bookstore or at the box office. Like I said before, with the sheer amount of films, television channels, apps, text messages, and magazines, you, as a content creator, have to immediately engage people's interest or they're moving on to the next thing before you have the opportunity to tell them about your awesome plot twist. If you can't hook them in five seconds, chances are you are stuck in low concept quicksand.

Don't rely on execution to be interesting.
Here's a film concept I came across not too long ago:

A man and his estranged father mend their relationship.

Is that an awful concept? Not necessarily. Given the right cast, director, writer, and producer, it could be an amazing, Oscar-winning, life-altering film. Just based on the concept and not knowing anything else, am I going to be tripping over myself to check it out? I don't think so.

What about a book about a man going through a tough divorce? Without knowing the author, I bet you're not pushing someone over at Barnes & Noble to buy it. With the right author and the right execution, it could be a book that makes Tolstoy jealous, but it doesn't have what screenwriter and pitchman Steve Kaire calls "obvious potential."

You want to desperately avoid a concept that relies on execution in order to be great. You need to develop a concept that is immediately interesting to the audience so their first impression of the project will begin to shade everything else. If you hook them right off the bat with one sentence, they'll be more forgiving if you don't execute to perfection because the coolness of the high concept has made them *want* to love it.

Above all, you want someone to say, "Why didn't I think of that?" This is always the hallmark of a great high concept story.

Moreover, in the independent arena, you want and need people to read your work and if you can hook them with a concept that is immediately engaging, you'll increase your chances of them actually reading it a hundredfold. And when I say "people" I'm not talking about your mom or your roommate. I'm talking about decision-makers, investors and other heavy hitters who tend to be so busy that the prospect of getting them to sit still for three hours to read something seems nearly impossible.

Opposites attract.

One of the most striking aspects of high concepts is how they generate interest by simply putting together opposites or things you wouldn't think go together. For example, take this concept:

> *A vampire hunter's mother is killed by a vampire, which fuels his passion for revenge.*

Eh. It could be great, but I'm not hooked. I think I'll pass or, at the very least, wait until I hear something more about it. But now let's stick an opposite in there to see how it punches it up.

> *Abraham Lincoln's mother is killed by a vampire, which fuels his passion for revenge.*

Wait — what? Abraham Lincoln hunting vampires? Holy smokes! I'm in.

Do you see the difference in those two concepts? Abraham Lincoln is the last guy I would expect hunting vampires, which is exactly why I want to see him (or read about him) doing just that.

Let's try another one:

> *A businessman falls in love on a business trip.*

Boring. Let's punch it up with some opposites.

> *An emotionally-stunted businessman falls in love on a business trip.*

"Falling in love" and "emotionally-stunted" are opposites, which help make it more interesting. But, at the end of the day, it doesn't completely hook me. Written by Tarantino, directed by Eastwood, and starring Brad Pitt? I'm there. Otherwise, I'm not jumping out of my seat to check it out.

Now, let's add in another opposite to see if it helps.

An emotionally-stunted New York businessman falls in love on a business trip to Los Angeles.

Okay, the whole New York/LA opposite dynamic makes it more interesting, but if I'm a tough Hollywood producer or book publisher, I'm not necessarily putting it on the top of my reading list. Let's keep working.

While on a business trip, a high-powered but emotionally-stunted Wall Street broker falls in love with a hooker from Los Angeles.

Now we're talking.

In addition to the emotionally-stunted/falling in love opposites and the East Coast/West Coast dynamic, you have the opposites of a high-powered Wall Street mogul and a prostitute from Hollywood Boulevard. Not only are their professions fairly opposite, but also their socioeconomic conditions. You can see how just adding opposites into a concept really helps strengthen the impact of just one line. Consider me sold.

Let's go through another example. What's more interesting?

An FBI agent goes undercover to catch a dangerous criminal.

or,

A huge, Austrian FBI agent goes undercover as a substitute kindergarten teacher to catch a dangerous criminal.

Putting together the opposites of "huge, Austrian FBI agent" and "kindergarten teacher" clearly makes the second concept more interesting.

Let's do it again. What's more interesting?

A man tries to solve the mystery of his wife's murder.

or,

A private investigator with no short-term memory tries to solve the mystery of his wife's murder.

Number two takes the day again because of the inherent irony of a private investigator who doesn't have any short-term memory. Irony is a high concept's best friend.

Knowing what we know now, let's take our initial concept and see if we can make it more of a high concept.

A man and his estranged father mend their relationship.

No obvious potential in my book, but I have faith in our ability to make it better.

A policeman and his estranged, ex-con father mend their relationship.

Police and criminals are good opposites, so we're moving in the right direction.

A policeman and his estranged father, who is still in prison, mend their relationship.

The fact the father is in prison heightens the police/criminal irony. Let's keep going.

A prison guard and his estranged father, who is incarcerated in his prison, mend their relationship.

Now they're even more diametrically opposed because of the son's profession.

Am I the only one who finds this fun?

Let's give it one more go.

A death row prison guard and his estranged father, who is an inmate on the same death row, try to mend their relationship the week of his father's execution.

Dang! Go back and read the initial concept and then read where we ended up. I'm telling you, opposites not only attract, but they also make your concepts significantly more interesting.

I was leading a story structure workshop for a group of high school students when one of the students, who clearly wasn't into the exercise because he was obviously too cool for school, made a smart aleck comment about what we were talking about. As a punishment, I made him come up with a high concept story on his own.

I told him to think of a character, but in terms of a profession more than personality. After some grumbling, he offered up the idea of a wizard — who had a pet dragon...with one leg (I'm not sure why it had one leg, but it did). So, I asked him where the least likely place for this fantastical wizard and handicapped dragon would be. His response was good — New York City. That brought him to the concept of:

> *A bumbling wizard accidentally flies his one-legged dragon through a mysterious portal and is transported to modern-day Manhattan.*

Honestly, he couldn't believe he put all that together and admitted to being proud of himself when he did. He should be because it seems like a fun story. To me, this has obvious potential, especially as a children's animated feature or a children's book.

Don't get me wrong. A high concept will still rely on execution to be good, but that's not what I'm saying. I'm saying a high concept won't rely on execution to be *immediately interesting* to a potential investor, producer, actor, audience member, or reader. If you achieve immediate interest with your concept, you'll still have to deliver the goods on the backend or your project will ultimately disappoint. We all saw this with *Cowboys vs. Aliens*, which was a fantastic high concept that made everyone say, "Why didn't I think of that?" and created a huge amount of interest and buzz, but ended up underperforming due to a lack of execution.

Can you see it yet?

Another great indicator of a high concept is the concept's ability to elicit a compelling mental picture. Great high concepts will paint the movie poster or cover art in someone's head.

Despite its execution or lack thereof, when I say, "Cowboys versus aliens," what do you see? Cowboys fighting aliens. When I say, "Abraham Lincoln: Vampire Hunter," what do you see? Lanky old

Honest Abe, tall black hat and sweet beard, going head-to-head with the Cullen Clan.

When I say, "Young woman going on a journey of self-discovery," what do you see?

Um... er... uh... a young woman... um... I got nothing.

The movie poster definitely isn't popping up in my mind's eye and I'd bet you a dollar one isn't popping in yours either. Even if I did form a picture, it's probably different than your picture, which is probably different than the guy-down-the-street's picture.

It's obvious this story is stuck in the dreaded low concept quicksand and is in desperate need of being saved. We'll let someone else save it, because we have quite a bit more work to get done.

Applying the high concept to a setting.

Now that you're familiar with what a high concept is, let's start using it in conjunction with people groups and locations. Again, with settings, we're thinking much broader than individual characters, considering locations, and now are putting together opposites in order to heighten irony. The setting for the ABC show, *Once Upon a Time*, is a great example of this combination.

> *A quaint, modern-day New England community where every fairy tale character ever created is living in exile.*

Locations? Check. People group? Check. Opposites? Fairy tale characters living outside modern-day Boston. Check. In this example, the location and the people group make up the opposite element of the concept.

However, the location and the people group don't always have to stand opposite each other in order to make up the ironic element of the concept. Let's come up with a setting from scratch to illustrate this.

Starting with a broad people group, let's choose "children." The opposite of a child would be an adult. An ironic situation to find children in would be a situation where the children made the rules, given that children are always the ones being told what to do.

How do we put it with an opposite to make a high concept setting? Simple.

A place where children rule society and reign over their adult counterparts.

Pretty interesting concept that has obvious potential, if I do say so myself. Notice that by putting the people group in an ironic situation, the high concept has come alive despite our not defining a location. With this concept as it is, you could choose a variety of locations to make it even more interesting and go multiple directions.

You could make it straight fantasy and have this be a magical land of children. You could make it a dramatic setting by giving it an alternate future, a post-apocalyptic backdrop. You could make it a real-world setting where these children have taken over an island after being shipwrecked, like in *Lord of the Flies*. You could make it a small-town horror setting like *The Children of the Corn* (in fact, this concept is what made *The Children of the Corn* so enticing to audiences). No matter what direction you want to go with the location, the fact that you built in irony through connecting opposites means you will always have a concept that can immediately attract attention.

I mentioned previously how in the *City of Refuge* project, we decided to use a small, country town as our setting. Clearly, a simple, small, country town is a textbook low concept setting. So, we started spitballing ideas on how to punch it up. The opposite of a small, country town? A big city. The people group who live in the town are nice, good-hearted, hard-working, church-going country folk. The opposite of that? Nasty, violent, nefarious, and cold-blooded criminals. The initial combination was both obvious and exciting:

A small, country town overrun by cold-blooded criminals from the big city.

There's a lot of story potential in that concept, which is a testament to the opposites and irony of location and people group working together to make the concept such a high one.

For our *Fury* project, we started with the location of a crazy, violent fighting arena for the setting, which we knew was perfect for the board game component of the franchise. But, a crazy, violent fighting arena wasn't a high concept per se, so we were forced to pair it with an opposite — an extremely peaceful, feng shui, cucumber-on-the-eyes, anger management retreat. This lead to the high concept of:

> *A reputable anger management retreat that takes its unwitting patients and forces them to fight for their freedom in an underground, neo-gladiator arena.*

This concept has a people group (anger management patients) and two locations (anger management retreat and crazy gladiator arena), with the people group ironically opposing the latter location.

These three elements of people group, location, and high concept make up the main body of your viable transmedia setting. If you nail these three, then numbers four through eight will be a piece of cake.

Don't forget your theme.

I know it's only one chapter removed, but this seems like a good spot to remind you to not forget your theme when you're building your setting. Remember, your theme makes up the creative borders of your project and anything that lands outside those borders will be scrapped.

Therefore, continue to ask yourself, "Does my setting facilitate and embody my theme? Will my theme be able to thrive in this setting?" If the answer is "no" to either question, you need to re-imagine your setting and allow your theme to inform your creative decision-making process in regard to your setting.

For example, in our *Fury* project, we wanted to show how being driven by pain and anger is ultimately destructive. Therefore, we knew we needed a setting that would highlight the topic of anger, which led us to this crazy, angry fighting arena. Once that location decision was in place, we started the process of defining people groups and mining for irony.

For *City of Refuge*, our theme of no one being too bad for redemption informed the choice of our people group, which was criminals. Once the theme informed our starting place, the location, the irony, and everything else were easy breezy.

Again, don't look at your theme as a limitation. Let it continually help and inform you of the creative direction you need to be going, especially in regard to your viable transmedia setting.

HERE'S A QUICK SUMMARY.

Creating a viable setting requires you to construct a living, breathing, multidimensional narrative world that has depth, history, and the potential to facilitate multiple stories across multiple platforms for many years to come.

A viable setting will allow your characters to thrive and is made up of eight distinct elements, the first three of which are:

1. *People Group* — Don't think in terms of individual characters. Rather, think broader, as in groups, labels, and types of people.

2. *Location* — Define a physical location for your setting. This could be as big as a galaxy or as small as one building.

3. *High Concept* — Using irony will make your setting concept immediately interesting to your fan base, freeing you from relying on execution to hook people. This is achieved by forcing opposites together.

HERE'S YOUR HOMEWORK ASSIGNMENT.

1. Look at the theme you wrote down at the end of the last chapter and express it or materialize it as either a location or a people group.

2. If your theme led you to a location first, define a people group who would be the least likely group to show up in that location.

3. If your theme led you to a people group first, define a location where no one would expect the group to show up.

4. If you're having trouble coming up with an ironic location for your people group, try devising a situation or a set of circumstances no one would expect the group to be in. In this case, once you have your ironic situation, go ahead and choose a location for your setting.

5. This will make up the rough concept for your setting. Go ahead and write it down.

CHAPTER THREE

TIME TO
FINISH
THE HOUSE

SOAPBOX, **VIABLE SETTING**, MACRO-STORY,
MICRO-STORIES, MULTIPLE MEDIUMS,
DYNAMIC CONNECTIONS, VERTICAL EXPLORATION

Broad Geographical Boundaries.

Now that you have the meat and potatoes of your setting, we can begin the process of enhancing, tweaking, upgrading, strengthening, and expanding your setting idea. I know I told you to make your location a definable one rather than a wide-open, generic backdrop; however, a consideration to keep front and center will be the actual geographical boundaries of your location, which is the fourth element of a viable transmedia setting.

As a general rule, the broader the geographical scope of your location, the more room there is to explore, which means more story potential.

Star Wars has an entire galaxy full of potential stories, whereas *Avatar* only has one planet. Therefore, simply because of the geographical boundaries of the concept, it would be easier to come up with thirty years worth of stories in the *Star Wars* universe than it would be in the *Avatar* universe.

Let's say you built a concept around a quirky coffee shop. Just looking at the limitations of setting, you may really be scrounging for stories because there is only a small amount of space to explore. I'm not saying it's impossible to tell a bunch of stories from a coffee shop, just that when you compare it to Middle-earth, you can see the stark difference and the difference is in the geographical boundaries.

If J. K. Rowling limited the *Harry Potter* setting to just the Hogwarts school building, it would have also severely limited the stories. By opening it up to the surrounding forests, lakes, etc., she gave herself more narrative opportunities and more freedom.

The small, country town of Always in our *City of Refuge* project necessarily has small geographical boundaries. Therefore, we were forced to broaden our concept to not just the small town of Always, but also the five neighboring towns and the surrounding forest as well.

Literally, the more room you have in your setting, the more you and your fans will recognize story potential, so, generally speaking, the bigger the better. However, I'm not saying it's absolutely essential to have an entire galaxy or a whole world in order for your setting to be viable. Once you get an idea of your setting, simply try your best to broaden your borders as wide as you can.

If your setting is a street, can you make it a block? If your setting is a city, can you make it a state? If not, so be it; however, if you can broaden the scope, future stories will more naturally spring forth simply because there is room for them to grow.

Map it.

Considering the geographical boundaries of your setting makes it very natural to start thinking of how your setting would look on a map.

The maps in the front of *The Hobbit* and *The Lord of the Rings* books do wonders in helping that setting come alive and can do the same for your setting. I'm not saying you need to become a cartographer, by any means. Just that mapping your world, considering landmarks and unique areas, brainstorming cool nooks and crannies and designing the major environmental elements will help solidify the concept in your mind. The more the setting is solidified in your mind, the more it will come alive to your audience.

SPECIAL SAUCE.

I'm going to make a bold statement. If you endeavor to come up with a completely original idea, new in every way, there's a 99.9% chance you're going to fail. I'll leave a 0.1% chance of God blessing you with an original idea, but outside of that, it's practically impossible to find a story that hasn't been told, a character that hasn't been written, or a setting that hasn't been used.

You may be thinking, "Dude, you're wrong. You've never seen anything like my idea before."

That's cute. Wrong, but cute. If I can prove that *The Matrix* is pretty much the same movie as *Monsters, Inc.*, I bet I can connect your idea to something that's been done before.

But here's the good news: we don't need to come up with completely original ideas in order for our projects to become successful.

If you're stuck on being completely original, you'll get frustrated and won't create anything. Rather, simply learn how to be fresh and clever and you'll save yourself loads of discontent.

Don't be afraid to start with ideas that have been done before. First of all, do it better (without getting sued, of course). Secondly, once you start putting in your own twists and turns, ideas, and new ways of doing things, you'll be amazed at how different it will seem.

This is what I'm talking about when I refer to the fifth element on the list — *special sauce*. This is simply adding some cool twists to an idea (in this case a setting) that has been used before.

Did the McDonald's corporation shy away from making a Big Mac even though other restaurants made and sold hamburgers? No. Why? The Big Mac is different because of the special sauce. Even though everything else on the burger is similar to other products, the addition of the special sauce makes the Big Mac unique.

So, just like the Big Mac, the idea you have for your setting needs special sauce to be unique.

The setting of *The Matrix* franchise is very similar to the setting of *The Terminator* franchise in that they both show a future where machines take over. Did that stop the Wachowskis from using the setting? Obviously not. So, how did they freshen it up? They added the whole "use the humans as batteries and keep them locked in a virtual reality" angle. That was their special sauce and it was so good, it didn't have a hint of being a retread even though James Cameron envisioned *The Terminator* setting fifteen years before *The Matrix* came about.

The *Firefly* franchise needed a special sauce to separate its setting from other franchises set in future space, such as *Star Trek*, *Star Wars*, and *Battlestar Galactica*. What's the special sauce? No aliens, a very distinct Wild West flare, and witty banter.

George Lucas designed his space setting with the special sauce of looking old and worn and actually being set in the past, instead of the future. That immediately set it apart from *Star Trek* and freshened the concept to a uniquely marketable level.

Transformers takes place in a setting where aliens crash-landed on earth. What's the special sauce that sets it apart from the hundreds of other alien stories that deal with a similar setting? The fact that these aliens are robots that can, well, transform into vehicles.

The concept of our *Fury* franchise immediately calls to mind films such as *Running Man*, *Arena*, *Gamer*, *Death Race*, and *The Hunger Games* because it plays on the concept of people being forced into a violent life-or-death competition against their will. We didn't let that deter us, though. We simply applied our special sauce: the psychological perspective that by experiencing pain and anger, people actually become stronger, better people. Therefore, by forcing the patients to tap into their own inner pain and rage, the antagonist truly feels he's not only helping them, but also doing the world a service.

In our *City of Refuge* project, we had the concept of a small, country town overrun by violent, big city criminals, but we needed a special sauce to take it to the next level. So, we added a neat legal twist. Instead of just simply being overrun by criminals, we turned the small, country town of Always into a legally sanctioned sanctuary city for criminals. Once a criminal crosses the border into the town, he can live freely within the confines of the town. If he crosses back over, he can be nabbed and punished for his original crime. This legal mechanism not only gave the town a stronger purpose, but it gave the entire project a special sauce that made it unique.

However, don't think it will always take a lot of special sauce to make your project fresh.

Stephenie Meyer simply made her *Twilight* vampires sparkle in sunlight instead of melting or burning or turning to ashes. It was a small addition, but it gave the genre a new twist and freshened up a concept that's been used hundreds of times.

In his remake of *Dawn of the Dead*, Zack Snyder freshened up a tired setting by simply making the zombies run fast — like freak

Olympic-sprinter fast. It wasn't a huge change, but it really made his setting stand out.

Figure out why?

One important thing, though, is to make sure your special sauce exists for a reason. Especially with our overly analytical culture, you can't just leave it with a "just because" answer.

If it's super science, magic, or unique political situations, force yourself to make them as credible as you can because if you don't, audiences will sniff it out in a heartbeat and write your project off as a big, fat cheese ball.

Watch the difference.

> *"Why do your zombies run fast when all other zombies I've ever seen stumble around like drunken hobos?"*
> *"Um, because they just do. Accept it."*

Lame. Also, you probably lost a fan. Good work.

Let's try it again.

> *"Why do your zombies run fast when all other zombies I've ever seen stumble around like drunken hobos?"*
> *"Because these zombies are being completely driven by their nervous systems. When their nervous systems kick into high gear, it overrides everything else, even their rotting muscles, and they end up running really fast."*
> *"Oh, okay. Cool."*

See the difference?

It doesn't matter that zombies don't actually exist. Just the fact that you're making it seem like they do requires some sort of explanation and justification. If not, you torpedo your own verisimilitude. Audiences want to believe, but you have to give them something credible to believe in.

If possible, build the "credible" justification into your project and dramatize it so the audiences won't even have to ask for an explanation. If it's not possible, at least be prepared to explain the justification of the special sauce at some point, because at some point the audience will throw a red flag and ask for it.

Play around with your rough setting concept and find your special sauce recipe. Once you have it, start applying it. You may need to drench your concept in it or maybe you just need a dash. Whatever the amount, use enough to make a concept that has been used before fresh, unique, and seem original.

Unfamiliarity.

The sixth element to apply to your high concept setting is a sense of *unfamiliarity*. Generally speaking, the more unfamiliar your setting is, the more the audience will approach it with a heightened sense of curiosity and anticipation and the stronger your initial hook will become.

Settings need to provide escapism and provoke imagination. You need to make me want to go to your setting and it's more likely than not I would rather not go somewhere I've already been a hundred times. Rather, I want to explore somewhere I've never been.

For instance, if I were to come across a film about a Midwest white boy growing up in eastern Kentucky in the 1990s, I'm not that interested. Why? Because I was there. I probably know everything the film will deal with and chances are I know it so well that I'll be able to pick out all the details the filmmakers actually got wrong.

Conversely, give me a book set in the Old West and I'm all over it. Why? Because I wasn't around during that time so I want to go, and because the book is set there, the author can take me.

This isn't to say that every setting you come up with needs to be rooted in fantasy or science fiction, or should be a period piece. A modern-day setting dealing with the fifty-eighth level Masons would be very unfamiliar to nearly everyone. I'm curious to know what goes on in that organization, so there's a greater chance your project will hook me from the beginning.

Armed with the understanding that the more unfamiliar the setting, the stronger the hook for the audience, let's quickly go through the following aspects of your setting and brainstorm ways to make them as unfamiliar as possible:

1. Location
2. People Group
3. Time Period

Location.

Is it possible to move your location to somewhere people aren't familiar with?

Obviously, if you make up the location completely (Middle-earth, Pandora, the world behind the closet doors in *Monster, Inc.*) you've maximized your unfamiliarity because the only person who's been there is you.

If you want to operate with more of a real world setting, however, can you give it an unfamiliar spin? J. K. Rowling set Hogwarts in Scotland, which would be pretty unfamiliar to most Americans, but maybe not to Europeans. So she made it set in a part of Scotland that regular, non-magic-wielding folks like us can't get to. Unfamiliarity score.

With our *City of Refuge* project, we tried to boost the unfamiliarity of a small, country town by pushing farther into the woods and changing it from just a regular small town to what is colloquially referred to as "holler" communities. These communities are farther set into the hills and are usually closed societies. Just a small change like that helped us boost the unfamiliarity of our location.

People Group.

If you want this aspect to be unfamiliar, you can create a brand-new people group or you can find an existing group of people most just don't know that much about, research the group, and go from there.

Invented people groups will tend to always be unfamiliar while existing people groups will vary depending on their exposure to mainstream society. Thus the difference between the familiarity of middle-class suburbanites and the familiarity of the fifty-eighth-level Freemasons I just referred to.

Actually, I'm not really sure if there are fifty-eight levels of Masonry, but you get my point.

However, if an invented people group has been done quite a bit in many other projects then even though they don't actually exist, they'll seem familiar.

For example, take aliens from outer space. Well, depending who you ask maybe they do exist, but presuming they don't, that group seems very familiar because it's been the subject of so many books and films. At the backend of the vampire trend, vampires now seem very familiar even though they would be an invented people group. This is where your special sauce comes into play.

Time Period.

The past is only as interesting as how far we're removed from it. Yesterday is less interesting than twenty years ago because I'm more familiar with yesterday than I am with what was going on twenty years ago. The more removed, the more unfamiliar.

The future, however, is unfamiliar per se simply because no one has been there — besides Marty McFly and Doc Brown, of course.

Of course, you can always cheat and do an alternate present, such as *The Walking Dead*. Sure, it's technically present day, but it sure as heck isn't the present day I'm familiar with.

There's no hard and fast rule.

The amount of setting unfamiliarity varies from project to project. Some people make all three of these aspects unfamiliar. When James Cameron created the setting for *Avatar*, he dreamed up a brand-new world and a new people group, and set it all in the future. *Transformers*, however, is set in modern-day (familiar time period) America (familiar location) and only has an unfamiliar people group (robotic aliens) in the mix.

You don't have to make all aspects unfamiliar in every way; however, you will need at least one of these aspects (location, people group, time period) to be high in unfamiliarity to ensure your concept's viability.

SETTING HISTORY.

The seventh and last element of a great transmedia setting is focused on your ability to get a *history* out of your newly created world. Similar to your setting needing geographical boundaries, the more history for your setting, the more stories you'll be able to extract from it moving forward.

Think about it.

American history books are just big, fat anthologies of stories from our setting's past (the fact that they're usually told in the most boring way possible is a whole other topic). If the US was only five years old, the history books would be much thinner because there wouldn't be as many stories to tell.

This is very similar to expanding the geographical boundaries of your setting. However, instead of enlarging physical locations to accommodate more stories, you're expanding the time surrounding your setting in order to accommodate more stories.

As a storyteller, you want the ability to move backward *and* forward in time. You don't want to get stuck just moving one direction on a timeline. If your setting is a school building that was built last week, you're not going to be able to mine for stories in the past and that will limit you creatively.

Can you tweak it to where the school was just started last week, but the original building the characters are using for the school is hundreds of years old? Just doing that could open your setting up to some interesting stories moving forward.

Think about setting and where you want to start. Make sure you can move backward on your setting's historical timeline as well as forward. If you can do both easily, you're doing yourself a big favor.

More history, more stories. More stories, more legs. More legs, more revenue. It's simple.

Segments and ladders.

A couple of more concepts to build into your setting are what we call social segments and status ladders.

Social segments.

Within your people group, there should be distinct *social segments* that, while easily distinguishable from one another with their own unique quirks and traits, generally exist on the same rung of the social ladder.

For example, in the *Harry Potter* series, the main people group consists of magic students. However, that group is further segmented into different houses — Gryffindor, Hufflepuff, Ravenclaw, and Slytherin — with each house having its own unique spin. Gryffindor is the house for loyal and courageous students, Ravenclaw is the house for quick-witted and book-loving students, Hufflepuff is the house for hard-working, diligent students, and Slytherin is the house for ambitious and cunning students.

The Hunger Games series used the same tactic when it made the creative decision to split the people group of the series into districts, with each district having its own unique connotation — the career-centric District 1, the technically apt District 3, coal miners of District 12, etc. Similarly, in our *City of Refuge* project, we divided our people group into six distinct, small, close-knit holler communities with each holler community having its own unique focus and personality.

Status ladders.

Status ladders basically incorporate a gamification element into the social segments. Not only is the people group segmented horizontally, but within the segments there should be different vertical levels of statuses held by the characters — basic social hierarchies.

You can find an example of this in *Pirates of the Caribbean*, where there is a very definite hierarchy on the pirate ships — slave, crew, first mate, captain, etc. As you can see, the characters in that setting can move both upward or downward on the status ladder without ever moving out of their social segment.

As I previously mentioned, J. K. Rowling incorporated social segments by having the sorting hat divide the magic students into houses. However, she also employed status ladders within the houses. First, you have the years in school (first year to seventh year) that initially build the status ladder. Additionally, though, starting in the fifth year of school, certain students are chosen as prefects — roles with special authority and responsibility. And even on top of that, a Head Boy and Head Girl are selected and lead all the prefects and, in many cases, the entire Hogwarts student body.

You could have this represented within a corporate setting with intern, associate, middle manager, director, and vice president. Or you could build it into a sports setting with a batboy, rookie, back-up, starter, and all-star. Any idea that allows the characters within a people group and within their social segment to either achieve more status or lose status they already have.

Why this is important.

While it may not seem essential to build these concepts into your setting at this point, doing so will allow you to reap tremendous rewards when you are building community and interaction in the later phases of the 360° Storyweaving Campaign.

I would wager that J. K. Rowling didn't fully understand what a popular creative decision building social segments in the *Harry Potter* series would prove to be. For years, fans have come up with ways to place each other into the respective houses. In fact, with the recent release of *Pottermore*, a special sorting system actually divides fans up into the houses. It has been probably the most powerful community-building tool for the franchise because it gave the fans a more tailored people group or set of characters to identify with. So, when fans who identify with Ravenclaw see a Ravenclaw character doing something awesome in the story, there's an added level of excitement and investment that takes place.

With the release of *The Hunger Games*, Lionsgate actually launched *TheCapitol.pn* website where fans could register themselves as citizens of Panem and receive their own District ID. As with the sorting hat function of *Pottermore*, the fans were assigned to a district and given access to their district's Facebook page. Once there, the fans could help their district receive Capitol favor and keep up with the district's stats and updates via the Capitol. This approach changed fans from simply rooting for Katniss to considering themselves a citizen and supporter of their district and connected them more closely to other fans who were also assigned the same district.

Assigning fans to different social segments (be it districts or houses) helps incentivize audiences to explore the world beyond the story of one protagonist, such as Katniss or Harry. It also encourages a group of people who never knew each other to rally around a common cause and participate in conversations and assets as a team — thus giving us that human connection and conversation transmedia always strives for.

Also, incorporating status ladders into the creative will also give fans the opportunity to achieve similar statuses in the Community Phase, partake in a richer experience, and strive for something. If the fans see characters going from citizen of a district to recruiter to mayor of the district to possibly president, that builds in a community activity for the fans to achieve those statuses as well.

Can't this wait?

Admittedly, these elements will have the most impact in the Immersion and Community phases because fans love them and use them as vehicles to further immerse themselves into the storyworld. However, that doesn't mean you have the luxury of coming up with these concepts after the Creation Phase is complete.

The only reason it's exciting for fans to be assigned to the Gryffindor house is because you see the characters of the books/ films being assigned there as well. The reason that being assigned a district has meaning is because it's built into the stories. It would be weird to introduce the idea of different houses for the fans if in the books or the films the characters are never actually assigned to houses. Doing so would strip the meaning out of the concept and would come off as a marketing ploy.

So, be sure to build social segments and status ladders into your settings and endeavor to make them a meaningful part of your stories. The more you do, the more you'll thank me when you get to the Immersion and Community phases.

THE FICTIONAL WORLD.

At this point in your setting creation, you can start mining your storyworld for depth and complexity. It should stand to reason that if you're creating a wholly fictional world you'll have more details to work out than if you have a regular earth-based setting.

For example, creating Pandora from *Avatar* presents more problems (and opportunities) than Gotham City in *Batman* because even though Gotham City is technically fictional, it's still governed by the normal rules of earth (physics, atmosphere, societal structure, etc.). Anything special about Gotham City, just like Hogwarts and the town of Always from our *City of Refuge* project, can probably be covered in the special sauce description. Pandora, however, warrants some special consideration because the entire planet doesn't exist. The same goes for *Star Wars*' Tattooine and even *The Happiness Factory* setting from Coca-Cola. This is what J. R. R. Tolkien called the development of the "secondary world."

The more unique details you work out for your world, the more it will come alive creatively and the less likely contradictions and continuity problems will pop up. You don't have to work it all out down to the atomic level. You simply have to make it believable for the fans. They want to set aside their disbelief, but if you don't at least present some plausible explanation for the most important and interesting details of a fictional setting, they'll ditch your project in a Na'vi minute.

Here are some special items to consider when creating your fictional world:

1. *Type*: Basically, what type of world is it? Is it terrestrial, a satellite gas giant, artificial, part of an asteroid belt? This decision will alter many things on your planet.

2. *Government*: Is the planet controlled under one government or many? Is it anarchy, tribal law, feudalism, competing states, etc.?

3. *Terrain*: What is the dominant terrain for the planet? Barren, cave, crater field, desert, forest, glacial, ocean?

4. *Gravity*: What is the gravity of the world? Light, standard, or heavy?

5. *Atmosphere*: Is the atmosphere breathable by humans? Do certain people need breathing suits?

6. *Hydrosphere*: Is your world arid, dry, moderate, moist, or saturated?

7. *Temperature*: Is the planet searing or frigid? If it's tide-locked it could be both.

8. *Length of Day*: twelve hours, twenty-four hours, thirty-six hours, two hundred hours?

9. *Length of Year*: seventy-five days, three hundred seventy-five days, five hundred days, six hundred fifty days?

10. *Population*: Is it sparsely populated, densely populated, or somewhere in between?

11. *Technology Level*: Is it mainly the Stone Age or is it super advanced?

12. *Sentient Species*: Who are the native species of the planet? Are there others who have colonized?

13. *Other Life*: What are the main animal species, as well as plants, bacteria, and viruses?

AND THERE YOU HAVE IT.

That's it. That wasn't so bad was it?

I know the last two chapters were beasts, but by now, you should have a really good understanding of how important a rich, deep, fleshed-out setting is to a story, especially if you want to be mainstream-compliant with a transmedia property.

Once you nail the theme and the setting, you'll find that everything else will begin to snap into place much more easily because the world you've created is now starting to come alive.

HERE'S A QUICK SUMMARY.

Creating a viable setting requires you to construct a living, breathing, multidimensional narrative world that has depth, history, and the ability to facilitate multiple stories across multiple platforms for many years to come.

A viable setting will allow your characters to thrive and is made up of eight distinct elements, the final five being:

1. *Broad Geographical Boundaries* — Literally, the more room you have in your setting, the more stories you will be able to tell. Try to get them as broad as possible while staying true to your vision and your theme.

2. *Special Sauce* — This is a twist that makes a conventional concept seem fresh and new. With the right amount of special sauce, your entire concept doesn't have to be 100% original.

3. *Unfamiliarity* — The more unfamiliar your setting is, the more curiosity and interest your audience will naturally have. Try to make your location, people group, and time period as unfamiliar as you can.

4. *Setting History* — The more history your setting has, the more stories you'll be able to extract from it moving forward. Make sure you can move backward and forward on your setting's timeline.

5. *Social Segments and Status Ladders* — Divide your character groups into different types and give them hierarchies. This will be beneficial in the Community Phase.

If you're building a fictional world, make sure you flesh all the aspects out completely. The more details that go into your design, the better off your world will be.

HERE'S YOUR HOMEWORK.

1. Take your rough setting concept made up of a location, a people group, and a high concept and force yourself to broaden the geographical boundaries of your location.

2. Go ahead and sketch out a rough aerial blueprint/map of your location.

3. Brainstorm a unique twist and apply it to your rough setting. This is your special sauce.

4. Take your location, people group, and the time period of your setting and make at least one of them extremely unfamiliar. Keep in mind, though, that the more aspects of unfamiliarity, the stronger the hook.

5. Build in social segments and status ladders for your characters.

6. If you're actually creating a fictional world, develop all the details that go into helping people suspend their disbelief.

7. Name your setting.

CHAPTER FOUR

WHAT'S THE STORY OF YOUR WORLD?

SOAPBOX, VIABLE SETTING, **MACRO-STORY**,
MICRO-STORIES, MULTIPLE MEDIUMS,
DYNAMIC CONNECTIONS, VERTICAL EXPLORATION

WHEW.

By now you've spent quite a few long, grueling hours laying the foundation for your project. It's been tough and challenging and even though your project is well on its way to being primed for mainstream transmedia success, your head probably hurts and you're probably fairly exhausted.

Hopefully, this has excited and challenged you at the same time. If you're miserable and resent me at this point, then maybe you should stick to being just a screenwriter, novelist, producer or playwright. :-)

But for those who are still up to the challenge, you're going to be stoked because we're finally getting back to familiar ground — actual stories.

We've leveled the ground, laid the foundation, and now it's time to start framing up this gigantic 90,000 square-foot house.

THEY CALL IT A STORYWORLD FOR A REASON.

There are many different terms for the collective narrative sandbox we're building. Some people call it a "universe," some call it the "grand narrative," and others call it a "storyworld." I tend to like *storyworld* because of the built-in story reference.

Thus, armed with a strong theme and a viable setting, it's time to ask yourself, "What is the *story* of my *world*?"

Again, we're thinking broadly; we're still looking down at the project from a Google Earth view (zoomed all the way out, of course). Therefore, when you're contemplating what the story of your world will be, don't just think of it in terms of a collection of historical events. If you did, they would look like they were just randomly scattered about on your setting's historical timeline with the only relation being they exist in the same storyworld and possibly have some character connections that work to unite them.

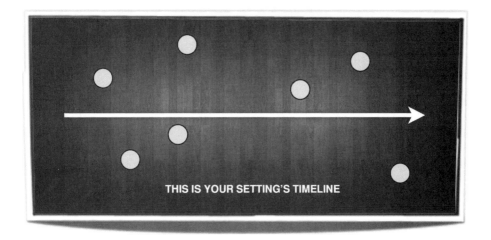

THIS IS YOUR SETTING'S TIMELINE

But to maximize the experience for your fans, you need something more cohesive and rewarding than simply random events peppered through the history of your setting. So, instead, think of your world's story as a collection of historical events *that thematically work together to tell the larger story of not a character, but of your entire setting or your world.*

Based on the previous chapter, you should have plenty of room to move back and forth on your setting's historical timeline.

Recently, there was a miniseries entitled *America: The Story of Us* that took all the major historical events of our country's past and wove them together in a riveting tale. Characters came in and out, different aspects of the country's history were covered, different locations were used, but it wasn't just a bunch of random events thrown together. Every historical event they covered played a role and had a purpose in the greater story, which allowed all of the events to work together to tell the macro-story of the greatest land on God's green earth (home team!).

This is what we call the macro-story and is the next step we're going to conquer. What's the difference, though, between a plain old collection of historical events and a true and well-designed macro-story?

Structure.

LET'S TALK STRUCTURE.

Ask anyone I know (or at least anyone I work with) and they'll tell you that I love story structure. From Aristotle to Robert McKee to Syd Field to Blake Snyder, I've always been a fan of those experts who have figured out how to use (and have taught others to use) story structure to maximize an audience's emotional reaction to a story.

Great stories aren't just collections of random events. They don't just meander around randomly and end whenever they want. Great stories are designed. They have purpose and direction and a steel skeleton that, if built correctly, will go unnoticed by the audience. It doesn't matter if it's a short story, a feature film, a video game, or a 400-page novel, understanding and utilizing story structure will do wonders in helping your story resonate with your audience.

With this understanding, we'll be taking your world's history, applying traditional story structure, and forming it into a macro-story that has rise and fall, action and reaction and conflict and resolution.

Using traditional story structure to re-imagine and inform hyperdiegesis is at the heart of the 360° Storyweaving Process and one of the biggest reasons this process is unique.

What the heck is structure?

I'm not going to presume everyone knows good story structure, so since the use of structure is what separates a macro-story from a random collection of events, I'm going to spend a few pages giving you a quick and easy primer.

A primer, though, is just that. You're not going to walk away from this chapter with a comprehensive knowledge of story structure. If you want that (which I highly recommend), we'll be publishing a dedicated book where we delve deep into the minutiae of the subject. Until then, go pick up Blake Snyder's *Save the Cat* series, Syd Field's *Screenplay*, Robert McKee's *Story: Substance, Structure, Style and the Principles of Screenwriting*, Viki King's *How to Write a Movie in 21 Days*, and Ansen Dibell's *Elements of Fiction Writing — Plot*.

These books are great and even if most of them are geared toward screenplays, if you're a story person and a writer in general, you should buy them... and read them... and read them again... and take notes... and read them one more time.

They're *that* good.

I remember being a senior in high school and wanting to enter a one-act play contest, but I didn't know what an act was. I asked my English teacher, but she didn't know either. Then, in a college playwriting class, I was marked down on a play because the professor said, "The same thing is happening throughout the whole play. It needs to go somewhere."

I responded with, what seemed to me, a very logical question. "Where is it supposed to go?"

He looked at me, almost confused. It was as if he was expecting me to react like all of his other students and try to argue that I was the next Tennessee Williams and that my play was impeccable. Instead, I immediately recognized the problem once he highlighted it and not only that — I actually *wanted* to fix it.

He sputtered, "I don't know, but it needs more structure."

Aha! Structure! This was what I needed so, excitedly, I asked, "Okay, so what kind of structure?"

"As in three acts."

It had come full circle.

"What's an act?"

He stood there for a second, broke eye contact, and said, "Yeah, that would be a good thing for you to research." And then he walked away.

Burn.

That would have been a great teaching moment for me and a wonderful opportunity for my professor to step in and actually teach me something of lasting value. But, alas, I was forced to continue on my apparent lifelong journey of trying to discover what an act was.

It wasn't until years later that I read Syd Field's *Screenplay* and finally had it explained. So, I took what I learned from him and read McKee's work. I took what I learned from both of them and read Blake Snyder's series. Then, I learned the Sequence Approach from Frank Daniels and then, coolest of all, I started adding my own ideas to the mix. Eventually, I ended up with a crazy story structure casserole that was exactly what I needed. I charted it out and what I was left with is the sheet you see on the next page.

I know what you're thinking, but don't freak out.

It's not as intimidating as it seems. Once you get over your initial reaction, you'll hopefully see that it will actually free you up to focus on story. Just like how street signs and mile markers guide you to your next spot when you drive, all of these plot points act the same. Like I said earlier, instead of toiling trying to figure out how to get from A to Z, you focus on getting from A to B to C and so on, until finally, you get to Z.

Good story structure acts like a skeleton. For example, I look nothing like Michelle Obama, but if you strip away every bit of flesh and tissue and just look at our skeletons, they'd look strikingly similar. In fact, you probably couldn't tell us apart because our skeletons (*cough* structure *cough*) are so similar.

But, in reality, we're very different. We talk differently, act differently, have different skin color, our personalities are different, we have our own quirks and talents — all the things that make us unique and special. If you're a good writer, you'll be able to cover up your skeletons with a constellation of uniqueness and originality, which will ultimately give all of your stories their own special breath of life.

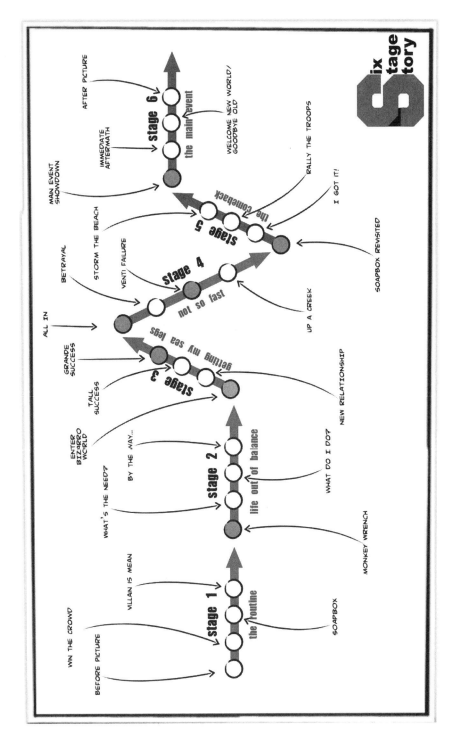

Story structure doesn't mean uncreative.

Some people say story structure is the antithesis of good, creative storytelling. Others say structure is for paint-by-number hacks, mindless, slavish screenwriting hordes laboring in the sweatshops of Snyder, Aristotle, and McKee. Structure is a "four-letter word" that spells death to art.

I wonder if there are factions of airplane designers who contend the laws of aerodynamics don't actually matter. I wonder if they push for tossing out those antiquated limits and restrictive laws such as thrust and lift that invariably result in every aircraft, no matter the size, looking shockingly similar, all possessing both motors and wings.

I wonder if they build neo-flying machines without regard for these laws, paint them crazy colors, ditch the wings, and give them weird bubble-shaped pods on the sides, toss out the motor and then try to take off.

And if they do, I wonder what they're thinking when their new-fangled flying machine doesn't fly, or worse yet, I wonder what they say when it crashes soon after takeoff.

The good news is a person actually doesn't die when a writer ignores story structure. The only thing that does die is the story.

Maybe it's because our society has been engineered this way. Maybe it's because people are just wired to respond this way. Whatever the reason, the vast majority of people respond to a good, solid skeletal structure.

If you think of it like a law, just like the laws of lift and thrust, your story will have a much better chance of taking off.

What is an act?

Traditionally, stories are broken into three *acts*. Some people break them in five, eight and even twelve, but traditionally it's three. So, what are the three acts?

At its core, Act I is normal life, Act II is crazy, bizarro life, and Act III is a blend of the first two acts.

Now how hard was that?

If I understood that when I was younger, I would have been ecstatic and much more productive in my writing.

One step further.

Once I developed my three-act sensibilities, I started to dissect it even further and ended up breaking down all stories to six distinct stages (see previous diagram). Each stage has its own singular purpose and uses four very simple story beats to achieve that purpose.

Let's make sense of the madness.

Trust me, we're still on the right path to design the macro-story of your world. We'll be using some of the beats on the chart to do just that. First, though, I'll need to go through each beat of the chart and take a couple of lines to define each one, highlight its purpose, and how it leads into the next section.

Stage 1.

Purpose: The Routine

This stage is meant to show normal, everyday life, as well as the hero's personal routine. It is the first part of Act I and should take up approximately the first 10% of your story. For a feature film script, it will wrap up around page 10. For a 300-page novel, this stage will finish around page 30. For a single 22-page comic issue, it will end around page 2 or 3.

1. **Before Picture:** Good stories are about change through character development. You know how a fitness infomercial shows a picture of someone horribly out of shape and then shows a picture of the same person after she got in shape? Well, this is the out-of-shape picture for your hero. This provides a visual starting point for the audience so that at the end of the story, they can judge just how far your hero has come. This beat highlights everything your hero needs to fix in her life.

2. **Win the Crowd:** You need for your audience to root for your hero, even if you want to use an unlikable hero or antihero.

Actually, *especially* if you want to use an unlikeable hero or antihero. Blake Snyder calls this the "save the cat" beat, but I always like to think of the film *Gladiator* when Proximo counsels Maximus by telling him, "I was the best because the crowd loved me. *Win the crowd* and you will win your freedom." You need your hero to do something that will make your audience love her or, at the very least, like her.

3. **Soapbox:** Revisit the first chapter and apply it to a story. This is the story's theme and is almost always tied to your protagonist's flaw(s). For example, if your theme is the only way to be happy is to be in a loving, committed, monogamous relationship, your protagonist's flaw could be she has an extreme aversion to commitment and love. This will naturally begin to build conflict in your story.

4. **Villain Is Mean:** This is the polar opposite of the Win the Crowd beat. Just like you need to get the audience to like your hero, you need them to hate your villain. Have your villain kick a dog, kill somebody, pick on a helpless person, ignore a geek at school, embarrass someone — anything to make the audience hate him.

Stage 2.
Purpose: Life Out of Balance

Stage 2 is meant to show how the normal life of the hero has been disrupted and how the hero responds. As the last part of Act I, this stage should wrap up about 25% of the way through your story. For a feature film script, it will wrap up around page 22. For a 300-page novel, this stage will finish around page 75. For a single 22-page comic issue, it will be around page 4 or 5.

1. **Monkey Wrench:** This is something that happens that throws the hero's normal life out of whack and starts the hero on the crazy path of the story. It's when Maximus' family is killed in *Gladiator* or when Olive gets the phone call from the pageant in *Little Miss Sunshine*.

2. **What's the Need?:** Soon after the Monkey Wrench sinks in, what the hero needs to do should be made clear. In *Taken*, after Bryan's daughter is kidnapped (the Monkey Wrench), the need is apparent — he needs to get his daughter back. The need should be measurable and visibly attainable.

3. **What Do I Do?:** Even though the need is clear, however, it's common for the hero to remain indecisive about how to pursue the need or whether to pursue it at all. Nevertheless, a decision to pursue the need must be made, transforming the need into a very distinct, measurable goal.

4. **By the Way... :** Many times after the hero decides to pursue the need, there's a surprise before entering Act II. For example, after Cinderella decides to get her magical makeover and right before she heads out to the ball, she finds out that (by the way) she'll turn back into her peasant-self at midnight. This isn't a necessary beat, but it's fun to throw in there if you can, since the more obstacles the hero has the better.

Stage 3.
Purpose: Getting My Sea Legs

Stage 3 shows us just how much the hero needs to grow and how, at first, the hero struggles adjusting to the upside down world of Act II. This stage should wrap up about 50% of the way through your story. For a feature film script, it will wrap up around page 55. For a 300-page novel, this stage will finish around page 150. For a single 22-page comic issue, it will be around page 11.

1. **Enter Bizarro World:** If Act I is normal life for the hero, Act II is completely upside down crazy life. Did you ever see the *Seinfeld* episode where Jerry and the crew played off the Bizarro character? If you didn't, you should. Bizarro is the polar opposite of Superman who lives on Bizarro-earth, the exact opposite of earth. So, moving into Act II, the hero makes the affirmative decision to move into not

only uncharted territory, but a world that is the opposite of the one from which she came. In *Star Wars: A New Hope*, it's when Luke leaves the farm on Tatooine and enters an intergalactic conflict. In *Legally Blonde*, it's when Elle leaves Beverly Hills to attend Harvard Law School.

2. **New Relationship:** The hero meets someone who is the perfect personification of the crazy bizarro world. Usually this will develop into a mentor relationship with the mentor helping the hero navigate the choppy waters of Act II. This is the Mick/Rocky Balboa relationship in *Rocky*, the Hagrid/Harry Potter relationship in *Harry Potter*, or the Morpheus/Neo relationship in *The Matrix*.

3. **Tall Success:** In the midst of the growing pains the hero experiences from being in the bizarro world, which shows just how much she has to learn in order to reach the goal and meet the need, the hero experiences a win. In coffee parlance, this isn't a big win, in fact it's pretty small, but it gives the hero a small amount of confidence. Typically, this win isn't necessarily tied to the main need or goal of the story, but is simply a result of being in the bizarro world. For example, in *Up* the need is for Carl to reach Paradise Falls and he enters the bizarro world of Act II when the house starts floating. The first obstacle Carl faces when he's in the air is to try and save Ellie's furniture from falling out of the house, which he does successfully. Notice, though, that saving the furniture isn't essential in getting him closer to Paradise Falls and is simply a result of the crazy world of Act II, which is the floating house.

4. **Grande Success:** This is a win that is, if you're familiar with Starbucks, a little bit bigger than the Tall Win. This win, though, is directly tied to the overall need of the story and actually brings the hero one step closer to achieving the goal.

Stage 4.

Purpose: Not So Fast

Just when the hero thinks she gets a hang of the bizarro world of Act II, things come crashing down around her. As the last part of Act II, this stage should wrap up about 75% of the way through your story. For a feature film script, it will wrap up around page 83. For a 300-page novel, this stage will finish around page 225. For a single 22-page comic issue, it will be around page 16.

1. **All In:** This is the midpoint of the story and the spot where the hero is no longer fighting against the crazy bizarro world. She accepts that she has flaws, which have been horribly exposed by the crazy bizarro world and her new relationship, and decides to embrace the theme set forth in the Stage 1 soapbox and change into her new self. Usually around this point, the stakes are also raised for the hero, just like when you go "all in" playing poker.

2. **Betrayal:** After the hero decides to embrace the change in her character, the bad guys really turn up the heat. The hero has experienced a couple of nice wins and has some confidence, but the bad guys expose the fact that she's not all the way there. At this point, either the hero gives in to weakness and betrays herself or she's betrayed by someone she has trusted in the bizarro world of Act II.

3. **Venti Failure:** This betrayal leads directly to one big, whopping failure. Because the stakes have been raised, it's about as bad of a failure as you can get and seemingly makes it impossible to meet the need of the story. In *How to Train Your Dragon*, this occurs when Hiccup lays down his weapons and tries to show the villagers that dragons are not what they think them to be. But when Stoick frightens the dragon and the dragon goes after Hiccup, Toothless flies from the canyon and comes to Hiccup's rescue in front of the entire village. Seeing the Night Fury, the Vikings take Toothless down and capture him.

4. **Up a Creek:** Now the hero regrets going "all in" because not only is it impossible for her to change, she's made things worse for everyone involved. Any friends she's made in Stage 3 are scattered and, at this point, it seems absolutely impossible to achieve the major need of the story. In *Miss Congeniality*, this takes place when the undercover operation is shut down by her superiors and Gracie Hart is left to find the pageant bomber by herself.

Stage 5.

Purpose: The Comeback

This stage moves the story into Act III and toward eventual resolution. The hero needs to pick herself up, dust herself off, and go after the villain and the story need like never before. This stage should wrap up about 90% of the way through your story. For a feature film script, it will wrap up around page 90. For a 300-page novel, this stage will finish around page 270. For a single 22-page comic issue, it will be around page 20.

1. **Soapbox Revisited:** Remember the soapbox we introduced in Stage 1 and the hero embraced at the beginning of Stage 4? After everything falls apart and it looks impossible, the hero must once again consider the soapbox and realize the value of change.

2. **I Got It!:** After a while of wallowing in self-pity and doubt, the hero figures out a plan and pulls herself out of the muck of depression.

3. **Rally the Troops:** Now that the lightbulb has gone off and the hero figures out a plan, she needs to pull together her comrades and friends she gained in Stage 3 and have been scattered by Stage 4, and convince them to rejoin the cause and go after the need. Alternatively, the hero may not seek out her friends, but they surprise her and show up anyway. In *Miss Congeniality*, Eric unexpectedly returns to help Gracie find the pageant bomber.

4. **Storm the Beach:** Using what she's learned in Act II from the bizarro world, combined with the ability she already possessed and took with her from Act I, the hero takes her plan and her friends and goes after the need once again.

Stage 6.

Purpose: The Main Event

This is the resolution of the story and will finally show whether the hero achieves the need of the story and how much the hero has actually changed through the story. This stage should take up the last 10% of your story.

1. **The Main Event Showdown:** This is the big showdown involving the antagonist and the hero, which is the biggest test of all. In *(500) Days of Summer*, this is when Tom goes to confront Summer at her party. In *The Empire Strikes Back*, this is Luke versus Darth Vader in Cloud City.

2. **Immediate Aftermath:** This is the immediate fallout from the Main Event Showdown. In *Titanic*, this is when Rose and Jack are floating in the icy water after the ship sinks.

3. **Welcome New World/Goodbye Old:** The hero tries to return to her old world, but it's futile. The hero has changed and now sees her old world differently. In *The Return of the King*, this is where the Hobbits try to go back to their Hobbiton pub and realize they don't fit in any more.

4. **After Picture:** We can now see how the hero has changed and all the flaws we discovered in Act I are now fixed.

Go watch a mainstream film or read a mainstream novel and you will start to pick out nearly all of these, right where they're supposed to show up. Make a game out of it even.

Again, this structure is scalable for short films, novels, even commercials and is very helpful for writers to learn and put to good use.

Using the fence posts for the macro-story.

Now that you have had a crash course in story structure, we're going to design your macro-story. However, we're only going to use seven of these beats to begin with, which we call *fence post* beats and which are depicted as the gray circles on the Six Stage Story diagram.

The fence posts include:

1. Monkey Wrench
2. Enter Bizarro World
3. Grande Success
4. All In
5. Venti Failure
6. Soapbox Revisited
7. Main Event Showdown

We call them fence posts because we feel they are the essential beats for a thorough and satisfying story arc, as well as a rewarding experience for your audience. Remember what your setting history looked like when the historical events were simply scattered along the timeline without any relation to each other beyond the fact they occurred within the confines of the setting? Well, by using the fence posts and forming a story arc, the story of your world will start to resemble an actual story.

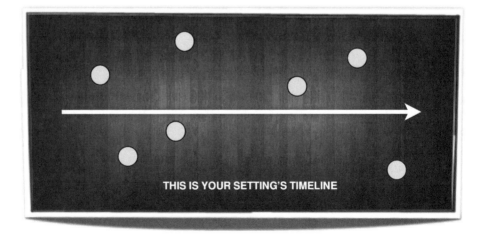

THIS IS YOUR SETTING'S TIMELINE

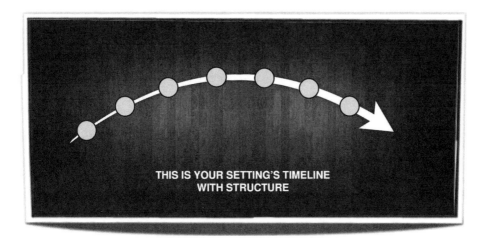

This changes the events from being random by giving each event a very distinct job to do and very pointed goal to achieve. For instance, instead of your first major event being whatever you want it to be, you know that since the first event is the Monkey Wrench beat, the event will need to throw the storyworld out of its normal existence and put it on a path of change.

For example, in our *City of Refuge* project the Monkey Wrench for the storyworld (which is the small, holler town of Always) is when the town finds out its patriarch has been hiding fugitives in an effort to change their lives for the better and decides to help. That's an event that fundamentally changes the town's path and future and is a perfect Monkey Wrench beat.

Designing the history of your storyworld in this way focuses you and changes your approach from trying to come up with an interesting idea from scratch to now presenting you with a simple creative problem to solve. To any writer, this should be a welcomed and empowering change.

Eventually, once you work your way through the process of designing the history of your world in accordance with the goals of the fence post beats, you'll see how nicely all the events work together with creative cohesion, coordination, and purpose. As a transmedia producer, I love looking at the individual piece of a macro-narrative and knowing its exact purpose. Like a good watch-maker, who knows the purpose and value of every gear and spring that works inside of a watch, I use a structured macro-narrative approach to communicating it to others, be it collaborators, investors, clients, or ultimately the audience.

Keep in mind that even though we start with just the seven fence posts, you're not limited to just those beats. Once you have the seven major beats sketched out, you can begin adding any additional beat you wish. We've simply found that it's easier to come up with the other beats after you have first framed up the macro-story with the fence posts.

This doesn't dictate order of experience.

The fact that you designed your transmedia project with a macro-narrative approach and pulled all your events and stories into one, big story arc doesn't dictate your eventual rollout schedule or the order the audience needs to experience your story. You can release it in whatever order you desire and the audience can experience the project in whatever order they desire and your story will have just as much impact.

Don't fall in the trap of thinking this negates the entire purpose of the macro-narrative story arc. First, think of it as a photo mosaic. Photo mosaics have a very specific and essential order to the individual pieces of art that work together to create the larger picture. If you mix up the order of the individual pieces of art, the individual pieces would be just as good, but there wouldn't be a bigger picture to be seen, just a bunch of individual pictures.

Alternatively, you can look at each individual piece of art in any order you wish, be satisfied with that piece, then step back and see the bigger picture the pieces work together to create. When this happens, there is an added level of excitement, reward, and satisfaction that you can't get in any other way. And how was this accomplished? A macro-order to the individual pieces, which worked together to create a bigger picture and broader experience independent of the order the individual pieces were viewed.

The beats of stories that employ nontraditional narrative structure, primarily flashback narratives, are necessarily experienced out of order by the audience. However, one of the most interesting things about the flashback narrative is that while it seems to be a complete deviation from the three-act model, in fact, each of the two stories (past and present) is structured according to the three-act model. Moreover, successful movement between the two stories depends on bouncing from one to the other at significant moments within the three-act structure.

Films like *Pulp Fiction*, *The Green Mile*, *Shine*, *Go*, *The Sweet Hereafter*, *American Beauty*, *The Usual Suspects*, *Citizen Cane*, *Memento*, and *The Big Chill* all present their beats to the audience out of order, but this doesn't alter the fact that each film still has a very strong three-act backbone. If you take these films apart and put them in sequential order, you'll see those backbones are disguised a bit, but are still very much in existence.

THE NARRATIVE SPACE ISN'T WASTED.

You'll notice that once you develop your fence posts, there is space left between each one of the beats. This is what we call "white space" or "negative space."

When designing a macro-story, you want a healthy amount of negative space. This will be important for two reasons. Firstly, it will give you room to continue telling new stories moving forward. Secondly, it will allow room for your fans to tell their own stories through fan fiction and what Scott Walker calls the "emergent narrative."

If one of your beats takes place on Monday and the next beat takes place on Tuesday, there's no room to tell a new story between the two. Maybe you can get creative and think of a cool way to tell a whole story over the course of an hour of time in your setting, but why make yourself work that much harder?

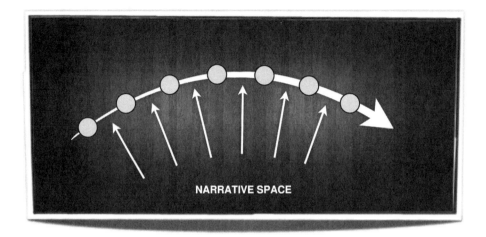

If one takes place on Monday and the other on Wednesday, at least you have Tuesday. However, if one story takes place on a Monday in 1914 and the next takes place on a Wednesday in 1927, you now see how you have much more breathing room to tell a lot more stories. And again, more stories equal more revenue, longer legs for the project, and a more rewarding experience for the audience.

WHAT HAPPENS WHEN THE ARC ENDS?

Does this mean the project is over? Short answer, no.

When, and only when, you've maxed out every single bit of narrative space and explored every cavern and crevice of all your stories, both horizontally and vertically (which will be discussed later), does the *arc* end. However, the end of the macro-story arc doesn't spell the end of the storyworld. It simply means that it's time to roll up your sleeves and design a new arc for your storyworld using new events that explore new areas of your world.

By this time, you will have built a very strong base, developed a large community, and will have the ability to continue to exploit new aspects and new stories of the environment.

Like Harry Potter?
Well, not exactly.

There was, indeed, an overarching story throughout the *Harry Potter* series; however, it wasn't a macro-story of the setting. Throughout the series, all the individual books and movies worked together to tell the story of the maturation and development of Harry, the rise of Voldemort, and their eventual showdown.

However, this arc was told independent of the setting and was very character-centric. As odd as it may seem, the Harry/Voldemort story is just a small part of the larger history of Hogwarts and the *Harry Potter* universe.

When you're designing your macro-story, as defined in this chapter, you're actually mapping out a larger history of the setting and universe. In the next chapter, we'll start mapping out storylines for individual characters, but right now we're still looking at the historical timeline of your setting from a Google Earth perspective.

THIS REALLY WORKS.

I can tell you from experience that this process will work wonders in scaling your storyworld up to a place where you can continue to tell multiple stories. It was shocking, even to us, how much it helped our *City of Refuge* storyworld.

Within hours of running it through this process, it began to morph and extend and grow, and what we ended up with is a pretty crazy Dixie epic that includes a state-sanctioned city of refuge for criminals, a war between six separate towns, and scores of criminal organizations. It was like it had a life of its own. We went from one television pilot idea to a more expansive setting, and close to fifty stories spread across ten different mediums, using over two hundred sixty different connections and over fifty unique characters.

There are actually some types of fish that grow to a size relative to that of the body of water in which they're living. The bigger the body of water, the bigger the fish grows. The smaller the body of water, the smaller the fish stays. Think of your story as this fish and your vision of the story as the body of water. What the 360° Storyweaving Process does is expand your mind and your vision so much, that all of a sudden, your story begins to organically grow right before your eyes.

Keep in mind, though, that through the process we didn't lose the small, character-driven story we originally wanted to tell. It's just snuggly fit inside a bigger, broader storyworld.

If you want your story to be bigger, just take a deep breath, continue through this process, and watch it grow.

Here's a quick summary.

The creation of a viable setting, or storyworld, begs the question, "What is the *story* of your *world*?"

It's your job to identify your setting's history and then tell a story using the setting's historical events, as well as a structured three-act story arc.

Think of your world's story as a collection of historical events that thematically work together to tell the larger story of not a character, but of your entire setting or your world.

Using structure helps you write because it turns you into a fearless creative problem-solver who is concentrating on getting from A to B to C to D to E to F and so on rather than getting from A to Z.

There are twenty-four distinct beats that appear in most commercially successful stories.

Seven beats are essential for structuring a bare-bones arc. These are called "fence posts" and include the Monkey Wrench, Enter Bizarro World, Grande Success, All In, Venti Failure, Soapbox Revisited, and Main Event Showdown beats.

Use the fence posts and their descriptions to design historical events that will ultimately make up the beats of your macro-story.

The fact the macro-story is in a traditional three-act arc will not dictate your eventual rollout schedule or the order in which the audience needs to experience your stories in order to be satisfied.

The narrative space between the beats will allow you to tell more stories in the future, as well as allow your fans to create their own content.

HERE'S YOUR HOMEWORK.

1. Think of your storyworld and setting in general — how it started and how it looked in the past, what it looks like today and what it will eventually look like in the future.

2. Using the description of the fence posts as strict guides, go into creative problem-solver mode and write out seven major events that take place in your setting.

3. Double-check to ensure that you've left a healthy amount of narrative space for yourself and for your fans.

CHAPTER FIVE

THE STORIES WITHIN THE STORY

SOAPBOX, VIABLE SETTING, MACRO-STORY,
MICRO-STORIES, MULTIPLE MEDIUMS,
DYNAMIC CONNECTIONS, VERTICAL EXPLORATION

BACK ON FAMILIAR GROUND.

Now that you've taken the time and effort to lay such a solid foundation for your universe by developing your soapbox, your setting, and your macro-story, this chapter is going to seem easy breezy. If the past few steps moved you out of your comfort zone as a writer, this chapter will move you back into your friendly confines by allowing you to reconnect with old friends such as protagonists, antagonists, plot twists, and character arcs.

Let's all take a collective sigh.

Good. Now, let's get back to work.

Before you start writing, though, we're going to:

1. Identify the subject matter of your **micro-stories**;

2. Decide on the new, unique aspects of your universe the audience will discover in each micro-story;

3. Flesh out your characters with a character breakdown; *and*

4. Work through the beats to develop an outline for your micro-stories.

WHY ARE THEY MICRO?

Well, simply put, they're called micro-stories because they're smaller parts of the macro-story that work together to form the macro-story arc we developed in the last chapter. It's like the macro-story is the engine and the micro-stories are the pistons, crankshaft, valves, and all the other parts that fit and work together to create it.

It's actually an important classification because the connections between the micro-stories and the macro-stories should be riveted in brass and the relationship is extremely symbiotic. The micro-stories collectively make up the macro-story and give it life, while the macro-story wrangles in the micro-stories and gives them both meaning and purpose.

You'll also discover a certain type of micro-story called a "nano-story," but let's focus on getting across the concept of a micro-story before we muddy our creative waters too terribly much.

Putting your macro-story to work.

How do you know what the micro-stories should be about? Much like everything else in this process, you're not going to be left to your own devices. When you're developing a huge cross-media franchise that relies on pinpoint coordination and creative cohesion, giving a naturally creative person complete liberty to develop any story he wishes is dangerous. It would be akin to putting a hyperactive child behind the wheel of an eighteen-wheeler; the kid can't be trusted and the big rig would be out of control, being much more destructive than productive.

Given ultimate creative freedom, you would probably come up with a hundred stories that would excel in quality, but lack in functionality. Although the stories may be good, I'd bet dollars to doughnuts they wouldn't coordinate with each other to tell the macro-story. So, as with the rest of the 360° Storyweaving Process, you have guideposts that will lead you completely through story creation and help you achieve the full creative potential of your macro-story.

The first thing you do to begin telling your micro-stories is to look at your beats to find the stories you need to tell. Remember when you developed the events of your storyworld based on beats a few pages back? Well, now it's time to put those events to work.

Simply put, these events will make up the heart of your micro-stories.

Dramatize the event.

The easiest way to accomplish this is to simply dramatize your event. Take your event, which was sketched out in a broad, Google Earth way, and start to personalize it by zooming all the way in to see the event on a more intimate creative scale. Now we start to see who the major players are in the event. Who is the hero? Who is the villain? What are the desires, plans, and motivations of each?

What are the obstacles that pop up to impede their progress? This causes the minutiae of the event to become alive and part of the overall conflict.

For example, in the macro-story of our nation, the 9/11 terrorist attacks would be a significant fence post event on our timeline. Accordingly, the films *Flight 93* and *World Trade Center* acted as dramatizations of that event. Through those films, 9/11 ceases to become just a historical event and becomes more relatable through the eyes of characters the audience cares about.

In our *Fury* project, one of our fence post events (the Main Event Showdown beat to be exact) on the macro-story timeline is when the Whitestone Wellness Institute's FURY Program is discovered by the authorities and exposed to the world. For the macro-story, that level of specificity is sufficient due to the very broad scope required for that particular step of the process. However, for the micro story, we begin asking questions such as, "How do the authorities discover the program?" "Who exposed it?" "Who are the people involved?" And so on. Therefore, in order to answer those types of questions, we needed to assign and develop a protagonist, assign and develop an antagonist, define a central plot, write set-piece action scenes — do all the things that make a good story. We did this and — bam! — we successfully dramatized a fence post event.

At the end of the day, this step simply requires you to take the events from your macro-story timeline and say, "Okay, I have to write a story about this."

Easy as that.

What about scope?

All your fence post events in your macro-story timeline should be significant; however, depending on your setting, your concept, and the amount of narrative history you've built into your timeline, the scale of your stories may actually vary. This, in turn, will alter the type of story you write for the event.

Let's take, for example, two events in the macro-story of America. The assassination of JFK is an extremely significant event in our history, though because it is relatively small in scope, it can be told very well in just one small story if one wanted. However, the American Civil War is also a very significant event, though its scale is much larger.

I don't think one approach to an event's scope is better than the other per se. It all depends on what fits your overall concept the best. This is presuming, of course, you took Chapter Two to heart and massaged, stretched, and expanded your setting as much as you possibly could, built in room for a good history, and did so with the understanding that a broader scope means there will naturally be more stories to tell moving forward (which is always a good thing). If after doing this, a grand, sweeping scope is best, then by all means go for it. Ultimately, this matters because, generally speaking, the larger the scope of an event, the more stories it will require to tell the whole tale competently and completely.

The question you need to ask when you're staring at a macro-story event in desperate need of dramatization is, "Can I communicate all the essential details of this story in a compelling way in a single story?"

If yes, then you're ready to start developing a micro-story. If no, then you'll have to divide it up into what we call nano-stories.

For example, what kind of story do you tell if you have a macro-story event like the Civil War occupying a single fence post beat? If this is the case, you can either defy the odds and tell one epic tale that would make Ridley Scott do a spit-take or you can break it up into nano-stories with each story telling a different piece of the war. I'd opt for the nano-stories.

Seriously? Nano-stories?

Yes, nano-stories.

"Nano" is smaller than "micro," so when deciding to distinguish between a single macro-event dramatized in a single story and a single macro-event dramatized in multiple stories, "nano" was the logical choice.

How many nano-stories should the event be broken into? I would suggest taking this process one level deeper and using the fence post beats again. This would give your event series an arc and ultimately give the event a richer treatment.

This actually creates a pretty interesting situation where you have a well-structured macro-story made up of stand-alone, well-structured micro-stories and possibly well-structured nano-stories. Every piece is structured. Every piece has purpose. Every piece directly affects the next.

It's enough to make me want to cry.

Not really. I'm not that much of a transmedia nerd, but it really does create an impressive architecture for a rich, thorough transmedia experience.

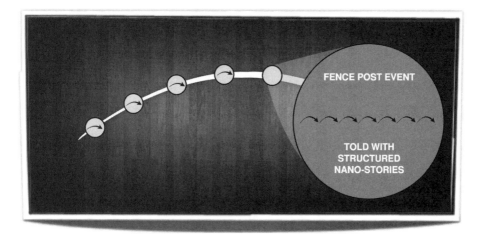

From this perspective, the entire *Harry Potter* series (which dealt with the rise and maturation of Harry and his inevitable showdown with Voldemort) could be considered a series of nano-stories that work together to tell the story of just one event in the entire *Harry Potter* macro-story. That means there are potentially at least six other epic series that could be told which would work with the original series to give the audience a complete model of Hogwarts.

Can you imagine the *Harry Potter* series we know and love being just one-sixth of the complete story? Maybe not before reading this book, but now you surely can.

Main plot or subplot?

When it comes to designing the plots of your micro-stories, you need to deal with the events that occur in your macro-story, but to what degree? Must the plot deal directly with the event or can the event be relegated to a subplot?

In general, the more the plot deals with the macro-story event, the better it serves the macro-story itself since more of the details of the event will be communicated to the audience. However, that doesn't mean a micro-story plot designed another way is completely off limits.

In our *City of Refuge* project, the Monkey Wrench event is when the small, holler town of Always finds out that one of its residents has been harboring fugitives in an attempt to rehabilitate them. It's a significant event that alters the future of the town and the micro-story directly deals with how this happens. The event *is* the plot.

Conversely, the Enter Bizarro World event is when the state legislature sanctions the practice and the town becomes a legally recognized sanctuary city for criminals. If we dealt with the event directly, the micro-story would have taken place in the halls of the state capitol and would have taken us out of our setting. So, we designed another plot that dealt with a completely different story and communicated the macro-story event through a television broadcast of the legislative hearings in which the townspeople were watching. We connected the new plot to the event enough to not make the macro-story event seem like it was an afterthought and it actually played out very nicely.

It reminds me of the *Mad Men* episode, "The Grown-Ups." The main plot deals with Don and Betty's marriage falling apart and Roger's daughter's wedding; however, the episode also deals with the assassination of JFK via subplot. This episode beautifully portrays that historical event as experienced by the fictional characters we've become so attached to. Through them we relive November 22, 1963, in impeccable historical detail, complete with actual news footage. The main parts of the event were communicated, but we never left our setting or changed the tone.

The event even directly impacted the main plot in that Roger's daughter's wedding was ruined. She, of course, is in tears. Half the guests, including a distraught Pete Campbell, don't even show up. Waiters are missing, there's no cake, and a lot of people obviously prefer staying glued to a television set in the hotel kitchen over celebrating the wedding. It was a creative decision that resulted in a great, great episode.

Ultimately, as a general rule, try to have your micro-stories deal directly with the macro-story event because it allows the audience to experience the event firsthand. If it's not workable for whatever reason, relegate it to a subplot and work hard to connect it to the main plot in a meaningful way.

Additive comprehension.

As you can probably surmise, this book isn't tailored toward writers who are only writing for the sake of writing. Of course we have to enjoy the process. Of course, we have to create something meaningful, but we also need to write so that other people will experience our art in a meaningful way *and* support the art through their purchasing power.

Before transmedia purists light torches and march toward my house, I want to be the first one to say monetary success cannot be the primary motivation for creating a 360° Storyweaving franchise. If it is, I guarantee you'll end up failing.

360° Storyweaving design should be intended to facilitate a rich and meaningful experience for your audience and ensure your theme will thrive in a convergent culture. However, we, as professionals (or amateurs desiring to become professionals), cannot let our artistic and thematic motivations push business realities so far down the list they're never truly considered.

So, I do not believe that balancing artistic vision with business strategy makes you a sellout. That's short-sighted, in my opinion, and is not a recipe for success. To me, that's just being smart.

And I like smart people.

So, while you're creating, be thinking about concepts such as market conditions, demographics, mainstream trends, etc. It will help you tremendously moving forward and increase your potential for getting consumers to purchase your stories and for building a loyal fan base.

Friction: our sworn enemy.

What then keeps consumers from purchasing a product? The dreaded *friction*.

Friction is a psychological resistance to a consumer doing what you want her to do (e.g., buy the book, buy the movie ticket, download the content), brought upon by a number of factors. These factors may include high prices, difficulty in locating the product, confusion, aggravation, boredom, lack of quality, and social stigma.

To make matters worse, designing a rich transmedia franchise will inherently bring about even more potential for friction because you're not just asking a consumer to simply purchase the book or download a song. Rather, you're asking them to purchase the book, then watch the movie, then download the song, then search for the web series on their phones, then visit a website and so on. With each added step, the friction increases.

While nearly impossible to completely eliminate friction, your goal is to minimize it as much as possible. Note that I said it's your goal as a content creator. Don't push this off to a marketing team or to some people who may be more business-minded. You, as the writer and creator, can do wonders in defeating the evil, snarling, trolling friction beast.

How?

Incentivize, incentivize, incentivize, and incentivize a zillion times over.

I'm not talking about coming up with gimmicky BOGO schemes. I'm talking about incentivizing creatively through your content and your micro-stories.

You need to incentivize your audience so much that they *want* to travel from story to story and platform to platform. You need to get them salivating (not literally — that would be gross) for the next component and have a burning desire to search, explore, and mine your storyworld for more and more.

You accomplish this through making your stuff really, really good (which should be a given) and by building additive comprehension into every single one of your micro-stories/nano-stories. And when I say every single one, I mean every single one.

Defined.

Additive comprehension essentially means that every micro-story needs to have a unique contribution to the unfolding story. Game designer Neil Young actually coined the term to refer to the ways each new text adds a new piece of information which forces us to revise our understanding of the fiction as a whole.

To put it simply, building in additive comprehension means that every micro-story in your project needs to include and communicate something new and unique about your storyworld that can't be found in any other story.

In a true transmedia rollout, there's no such thing as an urtext, a central place that holds all the information about your project. If someone wants to learn everything about your storyworld and about your macro-story, she'll have to experience all of your micro-stories. Thus, the incentive for exploring from story to story.

In *The Matrix* franchise, you can't learn everything about the concept and the world simply by watching the movies. Rather, you have to collect key bits of information conveyed through three live action films, a series of animated shorts, two collections of comic book stories, and several video games.

If you can hook the audience, they'll want to cross over to other stories (and take the time and pay the money to do so) because they'll want to learn more about the world, the characters, and the concept in which they've invested themselves.

The *Twilight* books, however, communicate the same information as the films, which communicate the same information as the graphic novels. So, as a casual fan, where's my incentive to continue to pay for the same information simply adapted to a different medium? Admittedly there's some incentive that naturally comes through the uniqueness of a different medium itself, but typically it's not enough to trump the friction that is keeping a casual fan from spending time and money. This is especially true in a recessive economy where there are tons of free entertainment options around every corner competing for consumer attention.

So, again, every single micro-story you write needs to communicate something new, fresh, unique, interesting, and original so as to incentivize fans to support it financially. Drill this into your skull because the concept of additive comprehension, my friends, is a foundational principle of any and all transmedia design.

Types of additive comprehension.

Now that we've established your micro-stories need to communicate some type of unique information to the audience, we turn our attention to the information itself.

Through our research, we've identified four types of additive comprehension that, when used to communicate information of significance, do wonders to incentivize audience members. They are:

1. New macro-story details;
2. Setting discovery;
3. Character comprehension; *and*
4. New micro-story details.

If you can, make sure every one of your micro-stories includes all four of these additive comprehension categories, and you should have no problem incentivizing audience members to continue the exploration process, thereby engineering an unparalleled creative synergy around your project.

Macro-story details.

In each micro-story you write, identify and spell out the unique information the audience will unlock about that macro-story event. This should be the easiest one to accomplish since your micro-story plots will closely deal with macro-story events. The more you deal with the macro-story event in the micro-story, the more information you will convey about the event and the more the audience will learn about the overall macro-story itself. If your macro-story event is the assassination of President Lincoln and your micro-story plot dramatizes the event from the perspective of John Wilkes Booth, the details of the event will naturally be communicated through the plot itself.

Additionally, you can also convey new details about a *different* macro-story event, though this shouldn't replace or overshadow the current macro-story event. For example, if another one of your macro-story events deals with the assassination of JFK and your micro-story plot dramatizes the investigation that followed, you could have your investigator discover a connection between JFK and President Lincoln, shedding additional and additive light on your previous macro-story event dealing with Lincoln's assassination.

Setting discovery.

This is when your audience gets to experience a new, unique part of your setting. Ideally this would be very much a "visual" geographic discovery rather than simply learning new details about your setting.

If in the *Avatar* sequel, we saw the exact same locations as we experienced in the first film, it still may be a great story at the end of the day, but the initial incentive to purchase the movie ticket wouldn't be as great as it could be. Apparently, though, the *Avatar* sequel will actually explore the underwater aspects of Pandora, which is something we didn't experience in the first film. Because it's something I haven't seen before, I'm more excited for the installment and more willing to shell out $12 to see it.

In our *City of Refuge* project, the All In micro-story is the only story where the audience will see the Juniper Bridge landmark, which is referred to many times throughout the other stories, but is never shown. Because the audience won't be able to actually see or experience this unique, interesting part of the *City of Refuge* setting in any other story, the incentive to check out the All In micro-story is exponentially higher.

Character comprehension.

Just like you want to discover new aspects of your setting, you also want to discover new things about your characters. If you build enough intrigue around your characters, your audience will naturally ask questions and will be willing to seek out the answers.

Where did your character come from? How did he get that limp? Why does she dress like that? Who are their parents? Why was the character in jail? How did the character learn how to do that one thing?

Joss Whedon did a masterful job of this in his ill-fated *Firefly* series and his development of the character Shepherd Book. Shepherd Book seems to be a mild-mannered preacher; however, he inexplicably holds some sort of high-priority status within the Alliance and on numerous occasions demonstrates a depth of knowledge in a number of fields one would not expect a clergyman to be familiar with. These include space travel, firearms, hand-to-hand combat, and criminal activity. In the fourteenth episode of *Firefly*, "Objects in Space," Simon berates the bounty hunter Jubal Early for assaulting a shepherd. Early replies, "That ain't a shepherd."

All of this worked masterfully to build a rabid desire for fans to find out more about the character and expertly incentivized the sale of the Dark Horse Comics series based on Book's past, titled *The Shepherd's Tale.*

Likewise, in our *Fury* project, there is a character named Macy in the feature film script who isn't who she says she is. In fact, you find out that Macy isn't even her real name, but you never actually find out her real name. We quickly discovered from people who read the script that her true identity, including her real name, was much-desired information. Because this created a great transmedia opportunity for us, we produced a song from Macy's perspective that revealed her backstory, her true identity, and, yes, her real name.

One of our creative team members actually has a son who at one time said he wanted to be a director one day. Knowing that, I would always encourage him to start reading feature film scripts since you can't be a great director until you truly understand stories on a script level. I encouraged him to start by reading our *Fury* script since he already had some familiarity with the overall concept. But, being a nineteen-year-old, he didn't want to take the three hours to read it.

Friction.

However, at his core, he's a music lover, so when we produced the song about Macy's character we had him listen to it. Because he latched on to the character's backstory in the song, he then wanted to read the script so he could find out what happened to her.

Do you see what happened there? We got a teenager to do something he previously didn't want to do and we did it with additive comprehension.

New micro-story details.

This type of additive comprehension will reveal a new piece of information about another micro-story in the franchise. For example, in the film *Clerks*, the characters Dante and Randal go to the wake of Julie Dwyer, who died in a swimming pool at a YMCA. In the sequel, *Mallrats*, which takes place one day before *Clerks*, the audience learns that she died from a brain embolism brought on by over-exercising before her appearance on the game show *Truth or Date*.

It adds color and sheds light on a plot point of another, related story and adds value to the audience's narrative experience.

Give us significance or give us death.

Not really, but you get my point.

It should go without saying, but I'm going to say it anyway so there won't be any equivocation. If you reveal insignificant information about the macro-story, the setting, a micro-story, or a character, you're not going to be stirring up the audience's desire to further explore your franchise and you're certainly not building the type of incentive required to overcome the friction of a recessive economy.

Sure, learning an insignificant fact about a supporting character in a micro-story is technically additive comprehension, but it's weak and will ultimately be chalked up as ineffective and as a missed opportunity. It's the difference between learning Bella's dad's favorite breakfast cereal in *Twilight* and learning how Edward became a vampire.

The more significance, the more value for the audience. The more value, the more incentive to cross over. The more incentive to cross over, the less friction plays a part in the decision making.

One and done.

One of the most important aspects of additive comprehension is the fact that the information that's communicated in the micro-story can't be found in any other story.

I'm not sure you understand the gravity of this. This means you can't ever use the information again. Ever.

Seriously.

If you communicate the same information in the feature film as you do in the webisode, where's the story incentive to see the feature film if you can just get the information with a click of the mouse?

In our *City of Refuge* franchise, one part of the setting we wanted to discover as a part of additive comprehension is a handmade tunnel system that exists underneath the city. It's a really cool part of the setting; however, when we made the decision to have the tunnels act as additive comprehension, that prohibited us from showing the tunnels in any other story we developed. We refer to them in other stories, but only show them in the comic series because that was a big part of the incentive to experience that particular story.

Alternatively, we could have opted to have the tunnels show up in other stories, though we would have had to earmark another geographic part of the setting for the fans to discover in order to satisfy the additive comprehension requirement.

TIMELESS CHARACTERS.

We've spent quite a bit of time developing the right stories, (both macro and micro) to tell. Now, it's time to develop the fictional people who will lead us through these stories by the hand — our characters. In the 360° Storyweaving Process, you can't have a macro-story without micro-stories and you can't have a micro-story without characters. Why? Because stories, like life, are about people and relationships. Likewise, drama is about conflict and conflict always comes down to people with opposing views.

At the end of the day, it's characters, more than plot, that grab an audience member's soul because characters have the ability to translate their own actions, desires, passions, fears, and dreams into the audience's databank of experiences and emotions. Our characters are our ears and our eyes on the ground of our setting. They're whom we root for and whom we relate to. After the intricacies of a plot fade, great characters will linger with a pseudo-physical presence.

The problem with most stories, though, be it screenplays or novels, isn't that the writer doesn't have an interesting character in mind. It's that they don't understand how to convey that character so that the reader sees what they see. So many writers believe that everything about their characters will magically emerge onto the page.

Not going to happen.

While there are books and workshops solely devoted to character creation, I've taken the liberty to outline a few strategies that, when used, help flesh out a character and build intrigue, depth, and interest around them.

High concept.

Do you remember our discussion about high concepts and how to use irony and "opposites" to build immediate interest in your concept, plots, and settings? Well, the same principle applies to designing characters. Simply put two opposites together and your character will immediately become more interesting.

How about a pilot who is afraid of heights? Or a hitman who becomes a pacifist? Or a schoolteacher who can't read? Whether you land on an extreme combination or a milder version, trying to build a high concept into a character will certainly help the character jump off the page much quicker.

Breakdown.

Many writers suggest developing at least a ten-page background/biography of your characters before you start writing. Personally, I think that's a great practice; however, I think before you try to punch out ten pages for a character, it's good to do a quick *breakdown* of all the characters. Once you have completed the breakdown, you'll have the framework to develop a more complete biography.

Here's a good primer on what to cover and include in a character breakdown:

1. **Name:** There are many literary and movie characters that become everlasting brands in our culture — Atticus Finch, "Ratso" Rizzo, Holden Caulfield, and Scarlett O'Hara, for example. Choose a name that is unique to your character and memorable to your story. The names should reveal something about your characters: who they are, where they come from, or where they are going.

2. **Archetype:** In Christopher Vogler's book, *The Writer's Journey: Mythic Structure for Writers*, he goes into detail about a number of classic archetypes that nearly all great characters fall into. Jeff Gomez is a big advocate of using archetypes in character design because it allows a character to resonate with what Carl Jung describes as the audience's "collective unconscious." One thing to keep in mind, though, is that you can have more than one character in the same role, and that characters often play more than one role throughout a narrative.

   - **Hero** — A character who is willing to sacrifice to achieve a goal.

   - **Mentor** — A character who provides guidance and tools the hero needs to complete the task.

   - **Threshold Guardian** — A character who acts as a barrier the hero attempts to pass through. These characters test the hero.

- **Herald** — An information-giving character who alters the life or goal of the hero.

- **Shapeshifter** — A character whose role and even personality change dramatically during a story.

- **Shadow** — A character who represents what the hero can become if the hero loses his or her way.

- **Trickster** — A character who majors in mischief and misdirection and usually straddles the line between hero and villain. Jeff Gomez has stated that Captain Jack Sparrow was originally designed as a Trickster archetype.

3. **Physiology**: What does your character look like to an outsider? Include things such as height, weight, clothing style, tattoos, noticeable scars, etc. Pretend like you're giving a description of a stranger to the police.

   - **A Great Description** — In this vein, a reader must get a sense of your characters after you've described them. Therefore, start considering the best way to initially present them to the audience. "Tall and thin" is boring. "Ichabod Crane on crack" evokes an image. Having said that, make sure the description matches the tone and genre of your story. I wouldn't use "Ichabod Crane on crack" in a drama, for example, but I might use it in a comedy. Here's a description of Christina in the original draft of *Source Code*.

   "*In contrast to the corporate suits around her, her appearance is thrift-store funky: black nail polish, dark lipstick, black hair with blue streaks, a button-down blouse edged in black funeral lace with silver skull and bones cufflinks.*"

   This description evokes a great physiological image of the character in our minds. Here's another great one from *The Adventures of Huckleberry Finn*.

"He was almost fifty, and he looked it. His hair was long and tangled and greasy, and hung down, and you could see his eyes shining through like he was behind vines. It was all black, no gray; so was his long, mixed-up whiskers. There warn't no color in his face, where his face showed; it was white; not like another man's white, but a white to make a body sick, a white to make a body's flesh crawl — a tree-toad white, a fish-belly white. As for his clothes — just rags, that was all. He had one ankle resting on t'other knee; the boot on that foot was busted, and two of his toes stuck through, and he worked them now and then. His hat was laying on the floor — an old black slouch with the top caved in, like a lid."

It's never too early to start thinking about how to craft a great description.

4. **Sociology:** This is how your character interacts with people around her or him. Does she have friends? Is he a black sheep? What kind of social circles does the character run in?

5. **Personality:** This is pretty self-explanatory. What's the psychology that surrounds your character? Is she trusting? Does he have an anger problem? Truly understanding the psychology of your character is key to finding his voice and determining what decisions he will make.
   One of the best ways to define your character's personality is to actually use a real personality test. Whether it's the Myers-Briggs test or the DISC assessment or another (you can find all of these and about a zillion more with a quick Google search), try to fit your characters into a defined category.

6. **Flaws:** A flaw goes a long way toward defining your character and should hold him or her back. The character will need to overcome a flaw in order to solve the big problems facing her or him in the stories. Rocky Balboa's flaw, for example, is that he doesn't believe in himself. This flaw is something that should come up repeatedly, something your character

should be bumping up against again and again. So in *Up in the Air*, for example, George Clooney's fatal flaw is his inability to get close to other people. That's why he's easily able to fire people. That's why he has meaningless sexual relationships on the road. That's why he barely talks to his family. That's why he gives seminars about the power of being on your own. At the very least, you should give your main character a fatal flaw. But I like to give a few of my secondary characters fatal flaws as well. It just makes them deeper.

7. **Goals:** Your characters need to have goals in order to stay active and moving forward throughout your stories. They need to want something. They need to be motivated. Without goals, characters become passive and boring and you cannot have a great micro-story with passive, boring characters. Moreover, character goals are great fodder for conflict because inevitably there will be characters whose goals are diametrically opposed. I suggest giving your characters two types of goals.

   - **Story goal** — This is the immediate, short-term goal the character has in any particular micro-story. In *Back to the Future*, Marty's goal is to get his parents together so he can get home. In *Taken*, Bryan's goal is to rescue his daughter. The story goal is directly tied to the plot of the micro-story and will change with every micro-story in the franchise.

   - **Life goal** — I don't think enough writers think about a character's life goal. Basically, it's the character's ultimate plan in life. Again, in *Back to the Future*, Marty's goal is to become a musician. It's not the most original or profound goal in the world, but it gives us insight into who he is. If his life goal was to feed starving kids in Africa, it would certainly alter our perception of the character. The life goal, as opposed to the story goal, should carry over into other micro-stories and should consistently shade the character throughout the franchise.

8. **Secrets:** Secrets always make characters more interesting and tell a lot about the characters themselves. Did your character kill someone and was never caught? Does she fear she's not good enough? The right secret can add a tremendous amount of depth to a character. Everyone has secrets — your characters should, too.

9. **Quirks:** We all have something about ourselves that's unique, so what interesting quirks and characteristics make your character stand out? In *Arrested Development*, Tobias is a "never-nude" and wears denim cutoffs in the shower. Does your character love to eat dry toast? Is she OCD? Does he collect action figures like Steve Carrell's character in *The 40-Year-Old Virgin*? Does he love marching bands? Does he wash his hands *before* he goes to the bathroom? One or two of these quirks can really liven up a character.

10. **Family Tree:** Who are your character's family members? Even if it's just immediate family members and you don't flesh them out, go ahead and sketch out the family tree. The difference in the personality of an only child and a seventh child is tremendous. Likewise, a boy who is raised by his grandfather probably has a different perspective on life than a boy who was raised by both parents. So the family tree can help shape your character's personality. Also, a family tree can be an extremely useful tool in a transmedia franchise because of the connections you can build between stories.

By sketching out a few sentences in each of these categories for all of your main characters, as well as key supporting characters, you'll already have a cast that will be jumping off the page even before you write the first words of your first micro-story.

A NOTE ON ROLES.

Traditionally, when developing a story, a writer will assign character roles such as protagonist, antagonist, supporting characters, etc. However, in the 360° Storyweaving model, we are forced to examine the characters in a more robust way.

Yes, every story will still have a protagonist, an antagonist, and a cast of supporting characters. However, because you'll be dealing with multiple stories, it's quite possible that the villain in your first story may become the hero in your third. A supporting character in one plot may be the hero of another and the hero of your film may be relegated to a background role in your comic book.

Because of this dynamic, every single character in your story-world needs to be interesting, developed, and well-rounded enough to carry his or her own story. In today's entertainment landscape, your characters can't be two-dimensional. People are complicated, so your characters should be as well. Therefore, give your protagonists secret dark sides that can possibly be leveraged in a villainous way in another story. Likewise, give your antagonists a few admirable traits and righteous motivations to make them more dynamic.

Your heroes will only be as interesting as they are bad and your villains will be as interesting as they are good. Every character has potential. Every character has a variety of personality traits, moods, and motivations. Sure, it takes more effort to develop your characters, but in the end you'll have a cast that is more dynamic and ready to be moved into whatever narrative role you need them to fill.

BRING BACK THE BEAT SHEET.

I'm sure you remember the twenty-four beats we listed in Chapter Three, as well as the crazy-looking Six Stage Story chart I developed for our creative team and internal projects. Well, now instead of just using seven of the beats as fence posts, as we did in the macro-story development, we're going to use every single one of them to ensure your micro-stories are as well-structured as they possibly can be.

Again, working through the beats is simply creative problem-solving and with the proper understanding of your characters and the information you need to communicate to the audience, developing your micro-stories should be a piece of cake.

Or pie. Whichever is easier.

I'm a pie man myself.

Take your characters and start working through the beats one by one and watch how the outline of your micro-story begins to come to life.

PUT ON YOUR SHOWRUNNER HAT.

Using our beat sheet for your micro-stories will help each story in your macro-arc stand alone. Remember to think of your macro-story as a photo mosaic rather than a puzzle. Having stand-alone stories will help create different (and stronger) entry points into the project and help appeal to different kinds of consumers.

Television showrunners have the never-ending task of ensuring their shows tell an overarching story (macro-story), but at the same time, have each episode (micro-story) stand alone. This helps the shows appeal not only to fans, but to people who come into the series late or who are simply flipping through the channels and just so happen to stop. They primarily achieve this balance through extremely tight, well-planned structure on both macro and micro levels.

In the same way, having well-structured micro-stories work together to form your macro-story will help your project appeal to more than just transmedia fans. Primarily, the 360° Storyweaving Approach will cause your project to be rewarding to three basic types of fans:

1. **Noncommittal Casuals:** These are fans who will experience a single story, but don't necessarily want to commit to any other stories. Just like moderates and undecided voters are always the groups that swing elections, capturing the support of Noncommittal Casuals will take your project out of the niche arena and propel it into the commercial arena.

When stories are self-contained, there's no sense of commitment to anything else, which appeals to the Noncommittal Casual (hence the name). As transmedia producers, we don't want to force fans to experience all of our stories in order to be happy and satisfied. Rather, if we make them happy and satisfy them with self-contained stories then maybe we can capture their imaginations and hook them. Once they're hooked, we incentivize (not force) them to explore the rest of the stories.

2. **Medium Geeks:** These are fans who will experience multiple stories, but are only loyal to one particular *medium* used in your project (comics fans, film fans, gamers, etc.) and have yet to experience any of the other mediums. What makes these fans happy? The fact that you've created an entry point into the project within their area of interest.

3. **Transmedia Fan Boys:** These are fans that will experience every story across every medium. These are the folks who will form your base and make your project thrive for decades. Be good to these people. Actually, be good to all people, but especially these. What makes these fans happy? The simple fact that you've created a quality, immersive experience across multiple mediums.

If you do your job like a good showrunner, you'll be able to appeal to, and capture, all three fan segments; however, if you don't have self-contained micro-stories, you're not likely to ever capture the elusive Noncommittal Casuals.

WHAT ARE YOU WAITING FOR?

Now that you know what your micro-story is going to be about, determined the new things you are going to reveal, created the characters who will star in them, and have identified a roadmap of beats to follow through the process, it's time to start punching out all of your micro-stories.

I would suggest using the beats to heavily outline all of your micro-stories before completely writing any of them. As you work your way through the outlines, new ideas will jar loose and your overall story will morph and change ever so slightly. When this happens, it's always easier to revise an outline than it is to rewrite a completed draft.

So, go ahead and outline to your heart's content. Once all your outlines are complete, you'll have a great layout of your entire 360° Storyweaving franchise and a great sense of the scope of the project.

Here's a quick summary.

Creating your micro-stories will consist of identifying the subject matter of your story, determining the new and unique aspects of your storyworld that will be revealed in each story, fleshing out timeless characters, and working through a comprehensive beat sheet to form an outline.

By dramatizing the events of the macro-story in the previous chapter, your micro-stories will collectively work together to tell the overall narrative of your storyworld.

If one or more of your macro-story events are so big in scope they can't be told with just one micro-story, use the fence posts from the beat sheet to begin developing a series of nano-stories that will collectively tell the story of the event.

Each individual micro-story needs to convey unique, meaningful information about the storyworld. This is called additive comprehension.

Additive comprehension incentivizes the audience to cross over and experience different stories and comes in the form of revealing new details about a macro-story event, discovering a new part of the setting, learning more about characters, and learning new details about another micro-story in the franchise.

Your micro-stories are only as good as the characters who star in them, so develop a character breakdown to ensure they are well-rounded and developed even before you start the writing process.

By using the complete beat sheet from the previous chapter, you will ensure that your micro-stories are as well-structured as they possibly can be.

Here's your homework.

1. Revisit the history of your macro-story and each fence post event and begin thinking of how to dramatize and tell the story of each event.

2. Identify the events that, because of scope, can't be told in just one story.

   - For those events, use the fence post beats to break the event into seven nano-stories. Identify the part of the event each nano-story will tell according to the purpose of each individual beat.

3. Jot down some plot ideas for your micro-stories using the macro-story events as the foundation of your main plot.

   - If absolutely necessary, relegate the macro-story event to a subplot and develop a different plot idea that connects to the macro-story event in a meaningful way.

4. Identify and write down the additive comprehension for each micro-story. In every micro-story, attempt to communicate new details about the current macro-story event, allow the audience to discover a new part of your setting, learn something new about a character, *and* learn something new about another micro-story in the franchise.

5. Identify the protagonist, antagonist, and major supporting characters for each micro-story and create a character breakdown for each one.

6. Begin heavily outlining each micro-story.

CHAPTER SIX

SPREAD 'EM!

SOAPBOX, VIABLE SETTING, MACRO-STORY, MICRO-STORIES, **MULTIPLE MEDIUMS**, DYNAMIC CONNECTIONS, VERTICAL EXPLORATION

If it doesn't spread, it's dead.

The marketplace is changing. People are different. Their brains are different. The new consumer doesn't purchase content in the same way our parents did and we, as producers, need to keep up. In fact, we are watching former Fortune 500 companies fold, even entire industries slowly implode, because they are tacitly refusing to learn how to navigate the chaotic waves of today's distracted, entertainment-overwhelmed, increasingly demanding consumer. In his eight-part blog series, Henry Jenkins writes:

> *"The role of the consumer or audience is in flux in this era of spreadable media. Consumers help to produce meaning around advertisements; they help to spread messages. Sometimes they are fans, sometimes critics. We are struggling to come up with a meaningful vocabulary to talk about these new sets of relationships."*

To stress the importance of designing stories imbued with multi-modality, he helped coin the phrase: "If it doesn't spread, it's dead." Multi-modality is just a fancy-pants way of saying in this day and age, we need to design stories that can be effectively and meaningfully spread into multiple mediums in order to be successful.

Essentially, to compete in today's marketplace our projects need to be like dandelions, whose seeds scatter in all directions when the wind blows, in order to create value and expand consumer awareness by dispersing the content across many potential points of contact.

Multiple mediums. This, friends, is the one thing all transmedia producers, no matter what definition they adhere to, can wholeheartedly agree on and is at the very heart of the transmedia concept.

In this chapter, I'll lay out the strategy for taking this academic-sounding concept of spreadability and practically applying it to your 360° Storyweaving project.

Also, just for fun, you should try dropping some of these Henry Jenkins phrases in public and watch people's reactions.

QUESTIONER: *So, what do you do?*
YOU: *Who me? Well, I design twenty-first-century entertainment franchises that combine radical intertextuality, multi-modality and additive comprehension, and are ultimately dispersed in commercially and culturally relevant mediums in order to create multiple and innovative consumer touch points.*
QUESTIONER: *You do what?*
YOU: *I'm a writer.*

WHAT'S WITH THE HOLDUP?

If transmedia, at its core, means spreading a story into multiple mediums, why would I wait until step five of the 360° Storyweaving Process before ever broaching the subject? Admittedly, there are some really creative, successful folks who actually like to *start* with a plan of how to spread the story into multiple mediums. They decide they want to use certain mediums, such as a feature film, web videos, a video game, and a comic issue, early in the process and many times before the concept is ever fleshed out. Then, these creative, successful folks write stories to fit that plan and those mediums. I'm not saying that approach is wrong per se, just that we do it differently.

I feel writing for a specific medium tends to limit your creative expression in a negative way because you're not totally focused on the story. You're halfway focused on the story and halfway focused on the functionality of the platform, and what almost invariably occurs is the lure of the bells and whistles of the platform leads you away from your focus like a siren on a cliff, making your story merely a secondary tool necessary only to show off your platform functionality.

Instead, at One 3 Productions, we design our stories to be platform-agnostic and simply focus on telling really good stories. Then after the stories are outlined, we take a step back, figure out what medium is the best match, and then start making the story fit the platform. Writing platform-agnostic stories gives you room to breathe and allows your stories to grow in meaningful ways you may or may not have anticipated.

The 360° Storyweaving Approach inherently puts story first in the process. By this time, you will have decided upon a theme, constructed a viable storyworld, developed a macro-story for the storyworld, and outlined multiple micro-stories that are connected in numerous and dynamic ways. It's been story, story, and more story. Now, at this point, we'll allow the organically delivered stories to inform us as to what mediums should deliver them to the masses.

Far too many transmedia producers start by thinking about the mediums and then watch in horror as their projects become more about the tech and the cool platforms than the story itself. Again, the creative, successful folks I mentioned earlier are able to start with their multiple mediums plan and still have a great project at the end of the day, but these people, unfortunately, are few and far between.

ONE DOOR IS NOT ENOUGH.

Traditionally, in the top-down model of entertainment, stories are handed down from the holy and exalted media conglomerates in exactly one medium of their choosing. This medium is, effectively, the only door through which fans can access this storyworld. It's presumed all fans, no matter what their interests or habits are, will want to go through the same door.

If enough fans squeeze through this one, single door, the suits will consider gracing us with a sequel or an adaptation into another medium (two new doors into the storyworld), both of which are more than likely going to be worse than the initial offering. If not enough fans squeeze through the door, the future doors will never materialize because the suits will say there are not enough fans to justify the risk.

Now, I'll be the first to admit that, for the most part, projects fail because the content simply stinks. However, it would be a logical fallacy to presume that everything that fails financially does so because the content isn't good. It could be due to creative timing, market shifts, the economy, poor marketing, or bad casting. However, it could also simply be because the suits at the studios or publishing houses didn't create enough doors for potential fans to enter into the storyworld.

The traditional top-down model of entertainment considers all fans to be fish in one giant sea when actually fans are more like fish separated by their interests into lots of tiny ponds. How do you catch fish in separate ponds? You cast different hooks into each one so you can pull them all into the same boat. Thinking all potential fans are going to respond to a story in one medium is as inconceivable as thinking you can catch fish in all the ponds by using one single hook. This simply denies the existence of human variability. Expounding on this analogy, start to think of traditional content creators as individual boats floating on the separate ponds. Necessarily, they can only catch fish in the ponds on which they're floating. Transmedia producers, however, put themselves in an advantageous position simply by standing on the ground between the ponds, from which they can cast their hooks into all of the ponds simultaneously.

EVERYONE DOESN'T LIKE EVERYTHING.

People are different and, thus, like different things. It's as simple as that.

Some people love movies, some people love comics, some people love video games, some people are avid readers and love to curl up to a good book, and to some people television reigns supreme. In the same way, there are some people who don't go to the movies or who don't have cable to watch television. There are some people who hate reading books and would rather simply listen to music or play a board game.

Given this fact (and, yes, I'm going ahead and declaring this to be fact), is it possible to create the magic bullet film or book or game that can break down all the barriers set up by factors like age, culture, interests, and gender?

I hate to burst your bubble, but don't plan on it.

If you figure it out, congratulations. Try not to spend your bazillion dollars in one place. But to everyone else, don't just throw one hook in one pond and pray for a miracle. Instead, actually embrace the fact that everyone doesn't like everything and plan accordingly. Of course, it never hurts to always pray for a miracle.

Perfect spaghetti sauces.

Enter Howard Moskowitz — a short and round man in his sixties who most often wears huge gold-rimmed glasses, and is a market researcher and psychophysicist who single-handedly innovated the spaghetti sauce industry.

While working for Pepsi in the '70s, he was tasked with figuring out the perfect amount of sweetener for a can of Diet Pepsi. Pepsi knew anything below 8% sweetness was not sweet enough and anything over 12% was too sweet, so Howard took the most logical approach. He whipped up experimental batches of Diet Pepsi with every possible sweetness percentage — 8%, 8.25%, 8.5%, 8.75% — all the way up to 12%. He tested all the batches on hundreds of people to see what batch was the most popular. Easy enough, right?

Wrong.

There was no clear victor because the data was all over the place. And then it hit him — finding the perfect sweetness for Diet Pepsi is just as impossible as catching the Easter Bunny. Why?

Because neither exists.

In the mid-'80s, he was contracted by the Campbell Soup Company, who was in the spaghetti sauce business. They owned Prego and were going up against the industry giant, Ragú, and desperately wanted to come up with the perfect spaghetti sauce. However, when Howard came into the picture, he brought with him the concept of plural perfection.

Openly declaring there was no such thing as the perfect spaghetti sauce, only the perfect spaghetti sauces, Howard designed over forty variations of spaghetti sauce that differed in every conceivable way — spiciness, sweetness, thickness, etc. When he charted what his focus groups liked, he saw everyone had a slightly different definition of what the perfect spaghetti sauce was. So, in the age when all spaghetti sauce was thin and blended, Howard talked the Campbell Soup Company into developing multiple kinds, including the then-unheard-of "extra chunky" brand. Not only did he find everyone liked something different, he also discovered once someone found a brand she liked, she was more apt to then try variations she wouldn't try before. The whole study was extraordinarily successful.

Today, it's difficult to appreciate how innovative this approach was to the food industry because now when we go to the grocery store, we see fifty variations of spaghetti sauce instead of just one kind. However, before Howard's innovation, the food industry was on the eternal search for human universals.

So, how does this apply to 360° Storyweaving?

If we know people like different things (which includes not only tone and genre, but also platforms and mediums), we should stop trying to push them out of their comfort zones. Instead, as twenty-first-century producers, we need to pull them into the project through doors/platforms/mediums they're most comfortable with, understanding that once we meet them where their interests lie, they'll be more apt to cross over into other mediums. This will be especially true when we incentivize them to do so with additive comprehension and dynamic connections.

Like I said before, when we were designing our *Fury* franchise, my friend's son said he wanted to be a director. When I heard this, I quickly offered to let him read our feature film script, telling him that was one of the best things a young director could do. But, being a nineteen-year-old, he didn't want to take the time and refused. Even though he said he wanted to be a film director, he really wanted to be a musician at heart. So, when we produced a song from the perspective of one of the more intriguing and mysterious characters in the feature script, which told the character's origin story, he listened to it immediately.

And you know what happened?

He asked to read the feature film script. He was intrigued by the character and wanted to find out what happened to her, so he took the three hours to actually read the script.

We went to where his interests were and opened a door into the project that was relevant to him. Once the story hooked him, we then incentivized him enough to cross over and do something he refused to do previously.

Behold, the power of transmedia.

Pretty darn cool, in my opinion.

When we embrace this very simple concept and design our transmedia project accordingly, we are empowered to create multiple entry points for audiences to be exposed to the project, and consequently, open the project up to many more demographics and many more markets that wouldn't normally be tapped.

Arranged marriages.

Have you ever heard there are certain types of people who shouldn't get married, such as two Type A personalities or a *Star Wars* fan and a *Star Trek* fan? Why? Because two driven, controlling, temperamental people will ultimately have a crazy, volatile relationship and the *Star Trek* fan will never get over the inevitable sense of inferiority that comes with, well, being a *Star Trek* fan (NERD BURN!). Ultimately, the differences are so inherent in the people that, outside of divine assistance, the relationships are all but doomed.

Likewise, there are certain types of stories that should never be put into certain mediums. Some stories make great films. Other stories make great video games. There are some that make great plays and even more that thrive as television shows. However, just because a story makes a great comic book, doesn't mean it will necessarily make a great film. Switching mediums is like switching spouses.

When you switch, the relationship will almost always be different, sometimes for the good and sometimes for the bad. Christine Weitbrecht (*christineweitbrecht.com*) calls this phenomenon *platform potency*, referring to how certain stories are more potent in certain platforms.

Therefore, picking the proper mediums to use for your project is a critically important step that should be strategic, well thought out and informed. This process, in a sense, is like choosing a spouse for your child. You wouldn't just up and marry your kid off to someone without knowing whether there was a good chance of the relationship being a great one. If you wouldn't do it to your child, don't do it to your micro-stories. Obviously, comparing a micro-story to a human life you created breaks down on quite a few levels, but you get the point I'm trying to make.

Before we haphazardly throw our micro-stories together with strange mediums, we need to pop the hood on these relationships and find out why certain stories fail in certain mediums and why others succeed. We need to define why certain stories can take advantage of a medium's unique characteristics and other stories can't. Those answers are there and they warrant both our examination and consideration.

As of the writing of this book, One 3 Productions is developing a veritable *Match.com* for stories where you can define certain characteristics of your stories and match them to the optimal medium. Since it's still in development, I'll simply list a number of considerations and factors for you to throw in the hopper when attempting to make this extremely important and strategic decision.

What are my options?

The first thing to understand when matching a micro-story to a particular medium is what platform options are actually at your disposal. I've taken the liberty of listing quite a few possibilities, but this list is by no means exhaustive.

Album

Backdoor Pilot

Board Game
Comic Series
Dice Game
Feature Film — Animated
Feature Film — Documentary
Feature Film — Live Action
Graphic Novel
iBook
Interpretive Dance
Journal
Miniseries
Mobile App
Novel
Novella
Paintings/Photographs
Poem
Role-Playing Game
Short Film — Animated
Short Film — Documentary
Short Film — Live Action
Short Story
Song
Spoken Word
Stage Play
Television Series — One Hour Episodic
Television Series — One Hour — Serialized
Television Series — Thirty Minute
Video Game — Console
Video Game — Mobile
Web Series

Some notable exceptions are social and online platforms. While they are absolutely viable storytelling platforms, because no one has truly figured out how to monetize them in a consistent way, they actually appear in the second phase of the Macro-Narrative Campaign.

Also, this list reflects those platforms that are, in my estimation, still commercially relevant today. You could, theoretically, tell a story across a series of stained-glass windows and, theoretically, monetize them by direct sales; however, because stained-glass sagas aren't actually popular (and by "popular" I mean "existent") in today's culture, they didn't make our list.

As an aside, this goes back to the soapbox we built early on. Because we want to communicate a very specific theme and message to people, it simply stands to reason we would then deliver the message in a medium that the most people use. So, look for the mediums that are hot and viable in today's market. What are the biggest revenue generators? Money isn't my sole motivator, but invariably where the most money is spent, the most people will be found. If you use a medium that has gone out of style and that many people aren't using in today's culture, it will only hurt the viability of your project.

What are the considerations?

Again, we're attempting to examine your micro-stories, and based on the natural characteristics of the story, we're going to allow them to inform us as to which mediums are the best to implement. By looking at the narrative characteristics of your story and cross-referencing them with the characteristics of the platform, we should be able to arrange the perfect marriage or, at the very least, keep it from being a complete disaster Hollywood marriage.

Here are nine considerations that should come into play when making these decisions:

1. **What's your overall project budget?** This consideration will narrow the field quicker than any of the others. While a console-based video game may be perfect for your micro-story, if you only have $5,000 in your project budget, it may not be a realistic option. Obviously, you can continue to develop the project and shop for future and additional investment, but the actual cost of the medium should continue to be a factor in your decision-making process.

2. **How visual is the micro-story?** If your micro-story is full of great visuals, you want to take advantage of it by pairing it with a visual medium. This would include anything designed for the screen (film, television, web series, video games, etc.), art-based mediums (comics, paintings, photographs, etc.), or the stage (dance or stage play). Non-visual mediums (novels, short stories, songs, or poems) won't take full advantage of your micro-story's visual potential, so if visuals are important go another direction.

3. **Is your micro-story high in action?** Your initial impression may be this question is the same as the last, but it's not. A micro-story can be extremely visual, but not be high in action, such as a story highlighting the majestic landscape of New Mexico. Likewise, your micro-story can be very action-oriented, but not rely on visuals. The visual mediums (*except* mediums such as paintings, photographs, or stage plays) will also work for this type of story. In addition, non-visual mediums, such as a novel, can work as well.

4. **How long is the micro-story?** If your story is going to end up being really long, you're going to need a long-form medium that will accommodate. Obviously, a medium such as a short film or a song wouldn't be a wise choice. A novel or graphic novel would be a great choice for an extremely long story or even a television series. Feature films ideally run just under two hours or around one hundred pages in script form, so depending on how long your story is this may also be an option. The same goes for a stage play. Of course, you can always get creative with your micro-story and split it into parts and go with an episodic web series or comic series.

5. **How complex is your plot?** Complex plots typically work best in mediums that allow for multiple perspectives, longer length stories, and more exposition. Novels are great, as well as feature films, graphic novels, and television series. Conversely, songs, albums, and poems don't work as well due to the length and the limited amount of exposition you can include. Folk songs are

known for their storytelling and if you listen to a few (such as Bob Dylan's "The Lonesome Death of Hattie Carol" and "Ballad of Frankie Lee and Judas Priest"), you'll see just how simple the plots need to be.

6. **What's the episodic potential?** If you know your particular micro-story has great potential for separate episodes, or if you were forced to take your macro-story event and split it into structured nano-stories, consider anything with "series" in the name — a comic series, a web series, a television series, a mini-series, or even a book series.

7. **Is your micro-story plot-centric or character-centric?** Character-driven stories work really well in mediums such as novels, films, paintings, and role-playing games, but not as much in video games or even comic books. There are examples of great, indie projects from the comic industry that are very character-driven; however, they typically are in graphic novel form and find difficulty piercing the mainstream comic demographic.

8. **Is your micro-story dialogue-heavy?** Certain mediums just don't accommodate dialogue as well as others. Mediums such as songs, poems, dance, painting, and games would be examples of these. Films, novels, web series, and stage plays would be examples of good matches. Find a medium that will allow your dialogue to flourish.

9. **How many characters does your micro-story have?** Lots of characters take up lots of space, so you'll need a big enough house to accommodate them all. Songs and albums aren't built for this. Neither are short films or even a web series. You'll need to move toward mediums like novels, films, television series, or even role-playing games to find a medium that can house your motley crew.

It gets really interesting when you have multiple competing considerations and sometimes, yes sometimes, you find you need to go back and tweak the story in order for it to find its home.

Again, this isn't a science (yet), but there are things to consider that will help inform you as to how to maximize the organic characteristics of your micro-stories, as well as the unique characteristics of your chosen mediums.

WHO'S DRIVING?

Despite the fact we're creating multiple points of entry into the project, not every entry point is equal. Inevitably, in every 360° Storyweaving franchise there will be one component that will stand out from the rest and act as the load-bearing wall of the franchise.

This is called the *driving platform*.

The easiest way to decide which platform will be driving your macro-narrative car down the road is to simply identify your core business. If you're a film producer, the driving platform will more than likely be a film. If you're a comic publisher, it will more than likely be a comic.

Another way to decide which platform should drive is to look at revenue potential. A feature film has a greater revenue potential than your web series component, so between the two, the feature film would be a better load-bearing wall for the franchise.

The major effect of a driving platform is that it will ultimately pull in the most people and will thus be the main springboard for fans to jump off and experience other micro-stories. The other micro-stories in all the other mediums will also be working to send the audience to the other components, including the driving platform, but because the driving platform acts as the biggest door into the project, it will demand special care and attention.

The driving platform should be the cleanup hitter in your transmedia lineup, stand out as the strongest offering of the franchise, be the biggest doorway for audiences to enter into the storyworld, act as the main jumping-off point for fans, and thus demand the lion's share of your marketing. It's a big role to fill, so make sure it lives up to the hype because if your load-bearing wall falls, the entire franchise will be damaged.

Obviously, the best way to ensure your driving platform is up to the challenge of leading your transmedia charge is to make sure you've written a great micro-story, ported it in the perfect medium, and maximized the functionality and unique characteristics of whatever medium you've chosen.

HERE'S A QUICK SUMMARY.

In today's media-saturated entertainment culture, content creators have to create as many entry points into a project as they possibly can. The way to accomplish that is by splitting your stories off into multiple mediums.

Everyone doesn't like everything, so if you can reach them in their area of interest or the medium of their choice, you'll have a greater chance to hook them and then to incentivize them to cross over into other stories and experience new mediums — possibly for the first time.

However, certain stories work in some mediums and don't in others. Once your stories are outlined into healthy treatments, you need to examine them to find their perfect mediums. Identify the dominant characteristics of your micro-story and match them to mediums that naturally accentuate those characteristics.

With a solid transmedia strategy in place, everything remains connected by the same central narrative and theme; however, each component should be tailored toward and excel at what its medium does best.

By identifying the story/medium combination that has the largest revenue potential, as well as the ability to draw in the most people, you'll also identify your driving platform. This particular micro-story will be the load-bearing wall of your 360° Storyweaving franchise.

HERE'S YOUR HOMEWORK.

1. Take your micro-story outlines and examine them in the context of these considerations:

- What's your overall project budget?
- How visual is the micro-story?
- Is your micro-story high in action?
- How long is the micro-story?
- How complex is your plot?
- What's the episodic potential?
- Is your micro-story plot-centric or character-centric?
- Is your micro-story dialogue-heavy?
- How many characters does your micro-story have?

2. Once you have responded to these questions, use the answers to help you match your micro-stories with mediums that will naturally accentuate them.

3. When your micro-stories have been successfully paired with the proper mediums, identify the match that has the most revenue potential and has the ability to pull in the most fans. This is your driving platform.

CHAPTER SEVEN

ALL HAIL THE
RAT
KING

SOAPBOX, VIABLE SETTING, MACRO-STORY, MICRO-STORIES, MULTIPLE MEDIUMS, DYNAMIC CONNECTIONS, VERTICAL EXPLORATION

Avoiding the franchise trap.

There's a nasty little lie going around that states if you tell multiple, self-contained stories within a creative storyworld then you're simply doing nothing but old, boring, traditional franchising.

That, my friends, is what you call a logical fallacy.

I'll freely admit the journey we've taken for the past one hundred-ish pages has taken us dangerously close to the edge of the gaping chasm o' franchising and if you sat the book down and never read this chapter, you and your stories would more likely than not fall in head first. But, thankfully, you're going to read this chapter and by the end, you'll have securely fastened yourself to a safety line and have figured out how to reap the benefits of a traditional franchise while simultaneously reaping the benefits of transmedia.

What's wrong with franchising?

Traditionally, the goal of creative franchising has been to build additional revenue streams by repurposing creative content. What's great about this approach? Profitability through added consumer entry points. What's wrong with this approach? Content is largely repurposed and, as you probably can tell, *repurposing* is an evil verb in transmedia circles, replaced by *quality story expansion*.

However, contrary to some opinions, this doesn't make franchising the sworn enemy of transmedia. Actually, in the commercial space, if transmedia attempted to come to blows with traditional franchising, neither would win. They're each strong and weak in their own ways.

What's great about transmedia, particularly East Coast transmedia, a transmedia technique that takes a single story and spreads it across multiple mediums? There's tremendous incentive to move from one platform and medium to the next. What's not so great about the transmedia approach? It's historically been difficult to monetize and make profitable.

[Begin sarcasm] If only someone would come up with a way to take the benefits of traditional franchising (profitability and

multiple entry points) and forge them with the benefits of trans-media (incentive), leaving behind the detriments of each. Boy, wouldn't that be something? *[End sarcasm]*

Seriously, though, this is a question of integration and incremental deviation from the established norm. More than likely, transmedia will not completely replace franchise development anytime soon. Likewise, traditional franchises are finding it increasingly difficult to engage audiences in a way that today's audiences demand.

This is called the 10% innovation method. You innovate by combining two differing ideas. Jelly is not brilliant. Peanut butter is not brilliant. But whoever it was that put the two together for the first time? *That* was brilliant.

The market is demanding a synthesis (*cough* 360° Story-weaving *cough*) and this book is the first step in providing it.

ALL HAIL THE RAT KING.

In the age of 24/7 media, iPads, PlayStations, and Netflix queues, it's difficult to build incentive and overcome friction with repurposed material. This is why we built sufficient additive comprehension between micro-stories. However, is the use of additive comprehension *enough* incentive per se?

Maybe, but the deck will certainly be stacked against you. This is especially true when you're trying to connect stories that are ultimately delivered across different mediums. Connecting a film, a comic, and a game in a way that it feels like one big story is more of a chore than trying to connect three films in the same way. With that in mind, you're better off employing a "belt and suspenders" approach, which means if additive comprehension is your belt, then **dynamic connections** are your suspenders.

Simply stated, the more you connect your micro-stories, the more they'll relate to each other and the more the audience will get the sense they are actually working together to tell one big macro-story. Henry Jenkins refers to this as *radical intertextuality* — making your stories relate to each other in a way that is far beyond the norm.

One man's radical intertextuality is another man's rat king.

You see, there's an old folktale about something called the Rat King. Rat kings are phenomena said to arise when a number of rats become intertwined at their tails and end up growing together to form one big, gross rat. Well, as horrific, nasty, and nightmarish as this is, we want our creative projects to have so many connections they form a rat king.

Admittedly, traditional franchising does employ some connections, primarily main characters and maybe some central locations. However, they're almost never enough to form the Rat King. We, as 360° Storyweaving producers, need to take it to the next level. We need more connections. We need connections that aren't passive and we need to connect our stories in new, different, more layered ways.

We need a rat king.

RECIPE FOR A RAT KING.

It's one thing to recognize your need for a figurative rat king, but it's a whole other thing to know just how many connections you actually need. In order to achieve rat king status, you need to make sure that:

1. Every micro-story plot is impacted by at least one previous micro-story plot;
2. Every micro-story plot impacts at least one future micro-story plot;
3. Every micro-story connects to every other micro-story in some way at least once; *and*
4. Every micro-story includes at least six different kinds of dynamic connections.

Confused? If so, don't sweat it. It'll all make sense soon.

The six different kinds of dynamic connections you'll utilize consist of:

1. Past-Plot Impact;
2. Future-Plot Impact;

3. Character Connections;

4. Location Connections;

5. Callbacks; *and*

6. Story Seeds.

Think of these connections as zip-lines for the audience to travel between the micro-story components. Looking at it in that vein, you need to make sure you don't move on to the next step until you have all six types of connections in every micro-story and each micro-story connects at least once to every other micro-story in some way. Using this approach will make incentivizing and crossing over between the stories much easier and much more rewarding.

And remember, this is the minimum of what you should include. If you can connect each story in four different ways instead of just one and you end up using thirteen connections instead of six, do it. The more connections the better. Once we put our *City of Refuge* project (again which simply started as one logline for a television pilot) through our magical 360° Storyweaving machine, we ended up with over 267 connections spanning nine micro-stories. Plus, as we continue the development process, I'm sure we'll add even more.

Nearly 300 unique connections sure ain't your grandma's franchise.

While Kevin Smith's foul-mouthed, irreverent *View Askewniverse* saga isn't a great example of holiness, it's actually a great example of using a large number of connections to connect six feature films, two short films, an animated series and twelve comic books. Smith definitely doesn't employ all the connections we're suggesting, but his stories are connected far better than most, so I'll be mining the saga (as well as some others) for illustrative examples of these connections throughout the rest of this chapter.

Let's go ahead and take a few pages to explore exactly what these connections are, how they work, and how exactly you can implement them.

Past-plot impact.

Your micro-stories should always be both impacting and being impacted by other stories in your storyworld. A micro-story should never be set apart as a silo. If it is, it'll eventually dry up and fizzle away and the potential of the micro-story will never be reached.

With the *past-plot impact* connection, your micro-story will *deal with an event or action that takes place in a past story's plot.* To get the full breadth and understanding of this connection, let's break it down word by word.

1. **Past:** The "past" in past-plot impact, refers to stories that take place earlier in your macro-story timeline and not actual rollout dates connected to your project.

   For example, in *Star Wars: A New Hope*, Luke is living on Tatooine and Obi-Wan is an old hermit in the desert. This is the direct result of the actions and conversations that take place at the end of *Star Wars: Revenge of the Sith*. This would be an example of a past-plot impact connection, despite the fact that *Revenge of the Sith* was actually released decades after *A New Hope*.

2. **Plot:** Simply put, this means the actual plot from the past micro-story needs to affect the actual plot in the current micro-story. Plot needs to affect plot.

   You may think this is pretty self-explanatory, but just because something happens in one micro-story and then impacts something in another micro-story doesn't mean the plots are impacted. What's the difference between a plot point and something else that takes place in a micro-story? A plot point alters the story, builds the conflict, affects the characters, etc. Anything else is just action.

   An unscientific way to decide if something is plot is checking to see if it's in your micro-story's outline. When you're drafting the outlines of your micro-stories according to The Six Stage Story diagram, you're boiling everything down to basic plot points. If it's worthy of outline inclusion and helps fill a beat, it's more than likely plot. In Kevin Smith's *Jay and Silent Bob Strike Back*, Jay and Silent Bob travel to Hollywood to shut down the production of the *Bluntman and Chronic* movie that is starting production. That is central to that story's plot.

In *Chasing Amy*, an earlier story in the *View Askewniverse* timeline, Banky Edwards starts to pursue more commercial goals for the *Bluntman and Chronic* comic series, which ends up being a bone of contention between him and Holden McNeil. Likewise, this is a significant storyline in that particular story. Plot affecting plot.

3. **Impact:** This speaks to the significance of the connection. The dictionary defines "impact" as, "the action of one object coming *forcibly* into contact with another." This means the connection needs to create meaningful change in the plot.

Again, the plot of every micro-story needs to be somehow impacted and altered due to the plot of a micro-story that is located earlier on your macro-timeline. The only minor exception to this is if your micro-story is actually the very first micro-story on your timeline. Obviously, since it's the first, there's no micro-story that takes place before it.

Future-plot impact.

This is simply the flip side of the previous connection, which means the plot of every single micro-story needs to somehow impact and alter the plot of a single micro-story located later on your macro-timeline. This means all of your micro-stories will be dealing with the past while also affecting the future. This is the most powerful way to connect your micro-stories.

Character connections.

Connecting characters is another great way to bridge the gap between micro-stories because the characters are our windows into the micro-story plots. There are actually three different kinds of character connections, which break down into the following categories:

1. **Personal Appearance:** This is when the same character personally appears in multiple stories.

The fact that Obi-Wan Kenobi, R2-D2, and C3PO all make personal appearances in every single *Star Wars* film helps the series maintain a creative cohesion and makes it feel more like one big saga than six separate stories. The constant recurrence of Jay and Silent Bob helps connect the six films of Kevin Smith's *View Askewniverse*, especially when the protagonists of the films almost always change. Also, the Nick Fury character appearing toward the end of the recent Marvel superhero films works to bridge the gaps between all the films as well as Joss Whedon's *Avengers* film.

2. **Personal Reference:** This is when a character from one micro-story is referenced in another micro-story.

As you can probably tell, this connection isn't as strong as the personal appearance, but can still help to connect different micro-stories. Kevin Smith's films also have a good example of this. In *Clerks*, we're introduced to the obnoxious Rick Derris, the consummate jock from high school who continues to brag about (and embellish) his sexual conquests. Then in *Mallrats*, Gwen Turner tells a story about a tryst she had with him at a party. Alyssa Jones does the same in *Chasing Amy*. So, even though Rick Derris doesn't actually appear in the other stories, simply referring to him works toward bridging the gaps between the films.

Moreover, if you read the *Spoon River Anthology* by Edgar Lee Masters, you'll see an expert example of how an author can connect a huge amount of characters. *The Spoon River Anthology* is a collection of short free-form poems that collectively describe the life of the fictional small town of Spoon River. The collection includes 212 separate characters, all providing 244 accounts of their lives and their deaths.

3. **Family Tree Appearance:** This is when a family member of a character from one micro-story appears in another micro-story.

The character Heather Jones appears as a minor character in *Clerks*, while her sister Trisha Jones appears as a supporting character in *Mallrats* and her other sister, Alyssa, appears as a major character in *Chasing Amy*. Even though it's three different characters appearing in three different stories, the fact that they're family members adds an extra element of cohesion. Similarly, the *Lord of the Rings* series wouldn't connect as well with *The Hobbit* if Frodo (the protagonist in the *Lord of the Rings* series) wasn't related to Bilbo (the protagonist in *The Hobbit*). There would still be connections, but this Family Tree Appearance definitely helps make the connection between the stories stronger.

Location connections.

Another way to connect your micro-stories is through the use of dynamically connected locations. Kevin Smith's *View Askewniverse* is centered on the towns of Leonardo, Highlands, and Red Bank, all located in Monmouth County, central New Jersey. This creative decision made it much easier for him to utilize multiple location connections. As with dynamic character connections, location connections can be utilized in a couple of ways.

1. **Reappearance:** This is when the exact same location physically appears in multiple micro-stories.

In *Clerks*, we're introduced to the infamous Quick Stop convenient store. Then in *Clerks II*, the Quick Stop is shown again. Likewise, in *Star Wars: Revenge of the Sith*, the dune sea of Tattoine is shown at the end of the film and then it's shown again in *Star Wars: A New Hope*.

2. **Reference:** This is when a location from one micro-story is simply referred to in a different micro-story.

Again, in *Clerks*, we're introduced to the Quick Stop. Then in *Chasing Amy* (which is actually based in New York), when Holden and Alyssa realize they both grew up in the same part of New Jersey, Holden mentions the Quick Stop. This isn't as strong as having it appear in the story, but remains a good option, especially when one of your micro-stories is removed from the central location of the rest of your stories, as was the case with *Chasing Amy*.

Callbacks.

A *callback* is simply a reference to an event that took place in a previous micro-story and the audience has the ability to go to the previous micro-story and see firsthand the event that was referenced. Again, "previous" simply means the micro-story is located earlier on the macro-story timeline and isn't referring to the order the stories are released to the public.

In *Chasing Amy*, Alyssa Jones mentions how her best friend, Caitlin Bree, had an unfortunate experience with a dead body and is now institutionalized. This actually occurs in *Clerks*, which takes place before *Chasing Amy* in the *View Askewniverse* timeline. If you hadn't seen *Clerks*, you could have gotten the DVD and watched the exact event to which Alyssa refers.

Remember, though, that it's your responsibility as a storyteller to inform the audience of the callback and educate them as to where they can experience the connection. If they don't know that a callback is, in fact, a callback, the connection is worthless.

Story seeds.

Story seeds and callbacks are nearly identical twins. Like callbacks, story seeds refer to events that take place in other micro-stories. However, there's one major difference between the two. Unlike with callbacks, the audience can't go and experience the referenced event because that particular micro-story has never actually been produced or released to the public. Because the audience members can't get their hands on the micro-story, the reference simply plants a seed in the audience members' minds (hence the name) and sets them up for a future story.

The most successful story seed in history was planted in 1977 by George Lucas when he wrote the line, "General Kenobi. Years ago, you served my father in the Clone Wars." When *Star Wars: A New Hope* was released, nothing existed about the Clone Wars. You couldn't find a book about them, a movie, a comic, a video game — nothing. But, it was provocative and it made you want to know who the clones were and why they were in a war.

Then, when Lucas announced he was going to release the Prequel Trilogy, the excitement for the film was off the charts, because that Clone Wars seed had been germinating for decades and was finally ready to harvest. Not only that, but he went on to release two more films, countless novels, video games, comic books, and an animated series — hundreds of millions of dollars of additional revenue — all from a single reference to a story that hadn't been written.

That, amigos, is a powerful story seed.

So, if Lucas can reap a harvest of this magnitude from one simple story seed, imagine what kind of harvest you'll reap if you sow at least one story seed in every single micro-story you write. Evangelist Jesse Duplantis once said, "If you plant year round, you'll always be reaping a harvest." This truth is equally applicable to spiritual law as it to 360° Storyweaving. Pretty cool, in my opinion.

But check this out.

As soon as the prequel trilogy was released, the reference to the Clone Wars in *Star Wars: A New Hope* instantly changed from a story seed into a callback.

Why?

Because the audience was then able to experience the event referenced in *Star Wars: A New Hope*. Why change the label? For the same reason we don't call a cornstalk a seed. Once a seed turns into a plant, it's no longer considered a seed. It's a completely different thing with a completely different function. Thus, the distinction in terminology will help you organize your project and differentiate between connections between actual micro-stories (callbacks) and connections between potential micro-stories (story seeds).

THE DRIVER IS SPECIAL.

Remember the driving platform from the last chapter?

Well, because you need your driving platform to drive the audience to all the other mediums, you'll need to ensure this micro-story connects to every other story in the most dynamic way possible. Therefore, the driving platform micro-story will need to:

1. Have its plot be impacted by not just one story that takes place before it on the macro-story timeline, but *every* micro-story that comes before it;

2. Have its plot impact not just one micro-story that takes place after it on the macro-story timeline, but *every* micro-story that comes after it; *and*

3. Utilize each of the remaining dynamic connections *at least* once.

You may find it difficult to rework your outline to accommodate all of these plot connections but if you do, you'll find your audience will be able to move from your driving platform to your other stories more quickly and easily, and with more incentive to do so.

So there they are. Six dynamic connections to help make your project into a giant rat king. By making sure you include every single one of these in every single one of your micro-stories and that you connect to every other micro-story at least once, you will ensure that your macro-story will actually feel and operate like one, big, timeless story and that new stories will continue to be birthed moving forward.

Here's a quick summary.

Traditional franchising has historically been a very profitable business model; however, it needs to be blended and integrated with transmedia to truly capture the attention of the YouTube generation. The combination of traditional franchising and transmedia will result in the transmedia approach to entertainment to become consistently profitable and lead franchises to thrive in the age of digital distraction.

One way to make sure your 360° Storyweaving project doesn't get mistaken for a traditional franchise is to apply a healthy combination of six types of dynamic connections.

1. **Past-Plot Impact:** The plot of every micro-story needs to be somehow impacted and altered due to the plot of a single micro-story that is located earlier on your macro-timeline.

2. **Future-Plot Impact:** The plot of every micro-story needs to somehow impact and alter the plot of a single micro-story that is located later on your macro-timeline.

3. **Character Connections:** The characters of multiple micro-stories need to connect in meaningful ways. There are three types of character connections.
    - **Personal Appearance:** The same character personally appears in multiple stories.
    - **Personal Reference:** A character from one micro-story is referenced in another micro-story.
    - **Family Tree Appearance:** A family member of a character from one micro-story appears in another micro-story.

4. **Location Connections:** The locations of multiple micro-stories need to connect in meaningful ways. There are two types of location connections.
    - **Reappearance:** The exact same location physically appears in multiple micro-stories.
    - **Reference:** A location from one micro-story is simply referred to in a different micro-story.

5. **Callbacks:** A reference to an event that takes place in a previous micro-story *and* the audience has the ability to go to the previous micro-story and experience the event firsthand.

6. **Story Seeds:** A reference to an event that takes place in another micro-story, *but* the audience *doesn't* have the ability to go to the micro-story and experience the referenced event.

HERE'S YOUR HOMEWORK.

1. Go through each rough outline you developed in the previous chapter and build in each dynamic connection *at least* once, while making a concerted effort to use even more.

2. Make sure the micro-story that is your driving platform has a past-plot impact connection to all micro-stories that come before it and has a future-plot impact connection to every story that comes after it.

3. Once your connections are made, start to turn your rough outlines into full, polished treatments.

CHAPTER EIGHT

UP, UP
AND
AWAY

SOAPBOX, VIABLE SETTING, MACRO-STORY,
MICRO-STORIES, MULTIPLE MEDIUMS,
DYNAMIC CONNECTIONS, **VERTICAL EXPLORATION**

Nothing is wasted.

I remember watching *The Thin Red Line* and being drawn to the scene where the camera dollies into the face of a dead Japanese soldier and the narrated thoughts of the soldier are heard. The narration closely parallels the earlier thoughts of an American soldier and opens the audience's eyes to a whole other perspective of that particular story.

I remember thinking, *Man, it would be cool to also see the whole movie from that kid's perspective.* The movie was already pushing three hours and while I wouldn't put it past Terrence Malick to make a six-hour film, I could see why they couldn't pull it off.

The fact that they didn't means that soldier's perspective was necessarily wasted.

When Clint Eastwood made *Flags of Our Fathers*, which tells the life stories of the six men who raised the flag at the Battle of Iwo Jima, I was fairly interested, primarily because Eastwood is an awesome director. However, I didn't have a compelling desire to see the film, so I didn't (at least not in the theater). When I heard about *Letters from Iwo Jima*, though, and about how it also told the story of the Battle of Iwo Jima, except this time from the perspective of the Japanese soldiers, I was fascinated. Watching the story of this battle unfold from two different perspectives gives you so much more of an understanding of the battle itself, but almost always these other perspectives and narrative pockets are perceived as "extra" and left out of the core narrative.

In fact, the term "cutting room floor" is an antiquated (but still tragic) phrase used in the film industry that refers to the footage not included in the finished film. I'll be the first to admit most of the unused footage is unnecessary, superfluous, or just plain old not good. But all too often there are exceptionally cool scenes and perspectives that are simply cut because of time.

Obviously, we don't live in a culture where filmmakers (outside of Peter Jackson) have the luxury of making three-and-a-half-hour films, where authors can channel their inner Tolstoy and write thousand-page novels, or where artists can release thirty-track albums, but that doesn't necessarily mean something like Johnny Depp's lost performance in *Platoon* or Kevin Costner's appearance in *The Big Chill* isn't worth seeing or can't add to the story in some way. It simply means there isn't time (or room) for it and when you're cutting down to essentials, quality narrative content becomes a regrettable casualty.

Since the advent of the DVD, directors' cuts and deleted scenes have attempted to bring these lost elements to the mainstream, but they almost always feel more like an afterthought than a legitimate addition or expansion of the story. Moreover, with the popularity of VOD services such as Netflix, which typically don't include special features, these elements are in danger of hardly ever seeing the light of day. For all intents and purposes, those unique pockets of the story are wasted.

Obviously, not everyone has an extra $13 million to go shoot an extra film like Eastwood and crew did with *Letters from Iwo Jima*; however, imagine if Eastwood took a more transmedia approach and released *Letters from Iwo Jima* in another medium — comic, novel, web series, television series, video game, etc. It would have acted as an extra point of entry into the story, given additive comprehension, and connected in multiple ways. It was ripe for an East Coast transmedia approach (spreading a single story across multiple mediums) and definitely could have opened up some new demographics for the film.

Regardless, it was cool to see a potential extension of a story not wasted and actually come to fruition to create a more complete experience for the audience. It'd be great to see more of this approach.

Enter **vertical exploration**.

With vertical exploration, nothing is wasted.

Since this subject can tend to get a bit confusing, I'll go ahead and give you a textbook definition of vertical exploration and we'll spend the rest of the chapter explaining it all. At its base level, vertical exploration is the process of taking nonessential (but still additive and rewarding) perspectives, scenes, sequences, or narrative pockets within a micro-story, separating them from the micro-story, and releasing them in a medium different than that of the micro-story.

Nowhere to go but up.

If you look back at the charts and graphics I've included in this book, you'll see the macro-story of your storyworld exists on a horizontal timeline. Because of the nature of time itself, timelines exist on a horizontal line because they chronicle one event after another, after another, after another and so on. When Henry Jenkins refers to spreadability, he generally refers to a story spreading horizontally.

So, for example, if you were to chart a timeline for the *Star Wars* films, it would look like this:

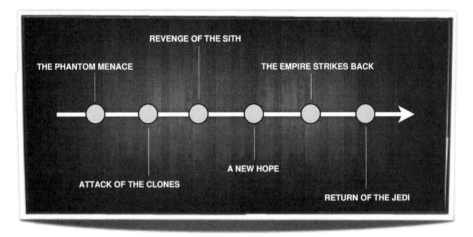

Each of these stories took place on a horizontal timeline that reflects the narrative history of the *Star Wars* universe. *The Empire Strikes Back* is further to the right on the timeline than *Attack of the Clones* because it takes place roughly thirty years later.

However, if you attempted to map the narrative universe of the *Letters from Iwo Jima / Flags of Our Fathers*, you'd discover something really interesting.

You can't do it the same way.

Why? Because the two stories occur simultaneously, stacked on top of each other in the context of history. However, the fact that they're stacked on top of each other actually informs us of the best way to map stories on a timeline that exist within the same narrative time block. If you can't map it horizontally, start mapping it vertically.

Think of it like New York City. When the New Yorkers ran out of horizontal real estate, they started building up, and up and up. That's the only way to fit a million and a half people on twenty-three square miles of land.

Using this vertical technique, the *Letters from Iwo Jima* and *Flags of Our Fathers* map would look like this:

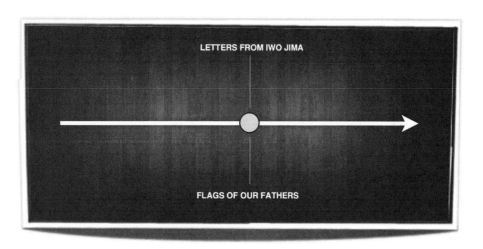

This is akin to what Henry Jenkins refers to as *drillability* or the process of occupying more of the audience's time and energies in a vertical descent into a story's complexities. Major crossover events in comics, such as DC Comics' *Blackest Night*, are a great example of overlapping stories that exist in the same narrative time and with different perspectives of the same events.

So, how does this help you?

Vertical exploration is the process of taking all those sequences, scenes, perspectives, and narrative pockets that are normally the victims of judicious editing and natural medium limitations and using them as additional tools to expand and promote your micro-stories.

Most importantly, vertical mapping and exploration of a narrative's macro-timeline visually reveals there are more layers of your storyworld to be exploited and more opportunities to explore. No longer will a great story element have to be cut for time, for a page count, or because it can't fit squarely into a beat. No longer will a great sequence be wasted on the cutting room floor. Instead, take it, map it vertically, and then split it off as its own individual story.

For example, in our *City of Refuge* album component, there is a sequence where a character flees from an unruly mob and runs into a church. The perspective of the sequence is from that of the mob and you watch from the outside while it sets fire to the church, burning it to the ground and killing both the character and the pastor inside. Because of the limited amount of space and time you have when producing an album, we couldn't fully explore what took place inside the church between the character and the pastor during the fire.

What did the character say to the pastor? What did they do when they saw the fire? What was the pastor's reaction? Since it's an interesting story that deserves to be told, we decided to split it off and have it as its own story. On our macro-story map, we had to map it vertically because it takes place during the same narrative time as the album story. When we split it off vertically, we could use the scene/sequence as an expansion of its parent story, which was our album.

Once you begin to find these narrative pockets in your micro-stories, split them off, and then begin to explore them vertically, you'll see just how many hidden jewels are buried in your stories. By themselves, they may not tell full-fledged, perfectly structured stories, but for this purpose that's not an issue. These stories are companion pieces to the micro-stories, therefore they don't need to be self-contained. Also, as you map your vertically explored stories, your macro-story map will begin to resemble a fish skeleton.

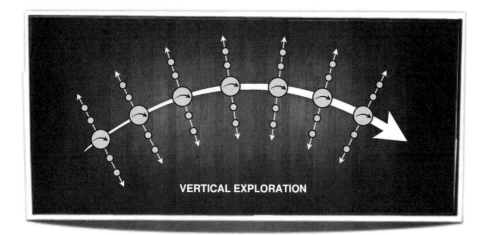

VERTICAL EXPLORATION

Not before, not after.

Not everything works well as vertical exploration, so it helps to have guidelines to more readily identify those ideal opportunities. First and foremost, to be a candidate for vertical exploration, the narrative pocket needs to take place within the same narrative space as a micro-story. This means it is a scene or sequence that takes place after the first page, but before the last, or after the first frame, but before the last frame. If it takes place outside these boundaries, it's not vertical exploration, but rather a separate micro-story.

For example, in the play *Hamlet*, I've always wanted to see how the dastardly Claudius killed King Hamlet. However, when the play opens, King Hamlet is already dead and his ghost appears to his son, Hamlet, ordering him to seek revenge on the man who usurped his throne and married his wife. Because the murder took place before the beginning of the play, it wouldn't be vertical exploration. Instead, you would need to build a full micro-story around this event and place it before the play in the macro-story timeline of the storyworld.

Likewise, in the television series *Sons of Anarchy* (which bears a striking resemblance to *Hamlet* — switch out tights for leathers, swords for guns, and horses for motorcycles and you have yourself a match) the death of John Teller takes place before the pilot episode of the series, so if you want to see how Clay kills John in order to take his place at the head of the table, you would have to tell a full micro-story rather than exploring it vertically.

Conversely, in *The Lord of the Rings: The Fellowship of the Ring*, Frodo is commissioned with taking the One Ring to the house of Elrond, who is calling together a special council. Legolas and Gimli both make appearances at the council and ultimately join The Fellowship, but we never see how Legolas and Gimli originally hear about the council or why they make the decision to attend. Since they both would have necessarily been notified about the council after the beginning of the story, thus happening within the same narrative space as the story, it would qualify as a vertical exploration opportunity.

Have you ever wanted to see what happens when Mr. White and Nice Guy Eddie go get the diamonds in *Reservoir Dogs* while Mr. Blonde cuts off the cop's ear? Perfect vertical exploration opportunity. In *Forrest Gump*, three or four years of Forrest Jr.'s life are skipped. Wouldn't you want to be there when Forrest Jr. asks about his real father for the first time? Vertical exploration allows for this opportunity.

So, again, if a scene, sequence, perspective, or narrative pocket is within the confines of a micro-story, it's a candidate for vertical exploration. If it lies outside the confines of a micro-story, it'll need to be developed as a micro-story itself, rather than a vertical exploration opportunity.

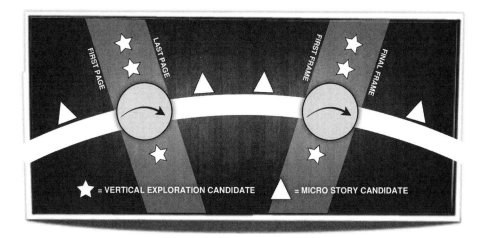

Why all the hubbub, bub?

The distinction between a vertical exploration opportunity and a micro-story is important because it will ultimately impact the amount of development you put into them.

As we discussed before, micro-stories need to stand independently, be tied to macro-story events, and be fully developed with beats and arcs and all that fun stuff. Vertical exploration opportunities, however, remain dependent on the micro-story for full comprehension and context and thus don't need to be as developed. Whereas the audience should be able to experience a micro-story and be completely satisfied with the experience without the other micro-stories playing a part, a vertically explored story should feel incomplete without also experiencing the micro-story it falls within.

Think of a micro-story as a responsible, self-sufficient adult who graduated college, pays his bills on time, and volunteers at the local animal shelter. A vertical exploration story is more akin to an eighteen-year-old hipster college student who lives in the dorm, listens to Sufjan Stevens radio on Pandora, comes home on the weekends to do his laundry, and still relies on monthly checks from Grandma to fund his daily burrito truck visits.

This isn't to say, however, that vertically explored stories should be completely art house or incoherent. They should still have enough plot, conflict, resolution, and character development to satisfy fans of the parent micro-story. Additionally, these stories should hook and adequately intrigue folks who haven't experienced the micro-story to actually seek out the micro-story.

THE USUAL SUSPECTS.

Once you've narrowed your search to the narrative space of a micro-story, you'll need to find those narrative pockets that will work the best. Because everything isn't worthy of being vertically explored, you'll need to focus your search for two types of opportunities:

1. **Another Perspective:** This is the *Flags of Our Father/Letters from Iwo Jima* scenario and is when you can shed more light on an event or a scene that takes place in the micro-story by telling it (or at least a piece of it) from another character's perspective; *and*

2. **Narrative Excess:** These are the story pockets, scenes, or sequences that are really good but, for whatever reason, couldn't be fit into the main micro-story.

However, while identifying these two kinds of narrative pockets is a good starting point for vertical exploration, the only ones that will truly be worthy of exploring will be those that are rewarding to the audience and additive to the micro-story in some way.

For example, take the scene from *Pulp Fiction* where Vince Vega and Mia Wallace are at Jack Rabbit Slim's and are having dinner. The scene is focused on the perspectives of those two characters. Technically, the scene could be told strictly from the perspective of Buddy Holly, their waiter and, technically, this would qualify as an another prospective vertical exploration opportunity. But would it add to the story at all or give us new insight into the characters or the plot? Probably not. Now, take the scene where Jules and Vincent retrieve Marcellus Wallace's briefcase from Brett's apartment.

Watching the scene, we see that Vincent is the one who flips the two locks and opens the case. Like Jules, we can't see what's inside, other than a small glow spilling out from the case. Vincent just stares at it, transfixed. After giving confirmation to Jules, Vincent shuts the case. Since we're given Jules' perspective in the scene, we don't see what's in the briefcase, though based on Vincent's reaction, it must be pretty amazing.

This, my friends, is a great opportunity for vertical exploration.

The contents of the case aren't necessary for the main plot(s) of the film, so I understand why Tarantino made the creative decision not to reveal them within the confines of the film itself. However, I can't be the only one who would love to know what the heck the glowing thing is in the case. A great way to reveal it is by creating a vertical exploration story where we see the entire scene from another character's perspective — Vincent's.

This would be both rewarding and additive and add an extra layer to the story for the audience without distracting from the pacing or the plot of the film.

On the other side of things, in our *City of Refuge* franchise, we have a micro-story where the primary location is the small town of Always; however, a major focus of the story is the result of a legislative debate that is ongoing throughout the story. The debate centers on whether to officially sanction the town's sanctuary program and the outcome will dramatically change the direction of the town. While we do show critical portions of the debate, the main plot concerns the son of one of the men who is testifying before the legislature. This necessarily causes the remaining, noncritical parts of the debate to become narrative excess and cut from the story. Nevertheless, hearing the entire debate will be a rewarding, additive experience since it will give more insight into the political climate surrounding the sanctioning of this controversial pilot program. This makes it a perfect candidate for narrative excess vertical exploration.

Also, have you ever wondered why the terminators look like Arnold Schwarzenegger and speak with an Austrian accent? In

Terminator 3: Rise of the Machines, a scene was cut that would have answered why Cybernet would ever create a race of ludicrously accented robots.

Did it happen within the same narrative space of the micro-story, *Terminator 3: Rise of the Machines*? Yes. Was it necessary for the plot? No, it was narrative excess. Would it be rewarding to see, adding a greater comprehension of not only the film itself, but the storyworld as a whole? Definitely, thus making it a viable candidate for narrative excess vertical exploration.

MEDIUMS REVISITED.

Once you identify good, rewarding, additive vertical exploration candidates, you'll need to start developing them accordingly. Again, you want them to be dependent on the parent micro-story for complete comprehension and context, but at the same time, you'll want to separate them from any micro-story so they'll be operating as even more isolated points of entry into the project.

For instance, similar to the previous Legolas and Gimli example, the audience also doesn't see how Boromir finds out about Elrond's secret council. It fits all the criteria we've detailed, which means it's primed for vertical exploration.

Peter Jackson must have recognized this as well because in the extended version of the film *The Lord of the Rings: The Return of the King*, he graces us with a scene where Boromir and his brother, Faramir, are celebrating a successful defense of Osgiliath. Grouchy old Denethor shows up and commands Boromir to attend Elrond's council, get Isildur's Bane, and bring it to Gondor to use as a weapon against Sauron. However, Jackson embeds this awesome slice of narrative excess inside the micro-story, which necessarily means it's not operating as an additional point of entry into the storyworld. If he had split that scene off, released as a separate piece of the pie, it would have certainly done more than simply operate as a mechanism to sell the extended version of the film.

Here's where it starts to get fun.

Not only do you want to split your vertical exploration story off as a separate point of entry, but you also want to move it into another medium. I know it sounds like I'm out of control, but if you put the vertical exploration story in a different medium, then not only will it operate as another point of entry into the project, but it will also pierce additional demographics and lead people who wouldn't normally experience the micro-story to do just that.

If you remember back a few chapters, when we were choosing the best mediums for our micro-stories, we were selecting from a list of mediums that are the most relevant in the marketplace and can actually generate additional revenue for you. However, when it comes to selecting mediums for your vertical exploration stories, feel free to get creative as the primary purpose of these stories is to market and promote your micro-story and not to become an additional revenue stream.

Any medium that is different from the parent micro-story is fair game. You want to take a vertical exploration story and print it on coffee mugs? Go ahead. Design it as a series of billboards? More power to you. Spread it across Twitter or other social media platforms? Fist bump coming your way. Just keep in mind the more obscure the medium, the less potency it will have as an additional point of entry, which means etching a series of illustrations on the sides of watermelons and selling them at the local Farmers Market may be pushing the creative envelope a little too much.

A great example of vertical exploration comes from Kevin Smith's *View Askewniverse*. In the film *Clerks*, Dante and Randall go to Julie Dwyer's wake. After they arrive, the scene cuts to them running out of the funeral home, being chased by Julie's family. We later learn while they were at the wake, Randall knocked over the casket, though because of budgetary cuts during the production of the film, they never actually filmed the scene. And I, for one, want to see it.

Within the narrative space of the micro-story? Check.

Narrative excess? Check.

Additive or rewarding? Check.

So, what did the good Mr. Smith do? He split it off from the micro-story and released the missing scene in a different medium than the micro-story. In this case, it was as an animated short.

A beautiful example of vertical exploration.

KEEP FEEDING THE RAT KING.

As you should recall, the Rat King is made up of dynamic connections and though your vertical explorations will necessarily be connected to their parent micro-story, that's not going to suffice.

The Rat King demands more.

And you should, too. Again, whenever you build a dynamic connection, you build a road from one story to another, which makes it easier for your audience to cross over and experience more and more of your storyworld.

Given that, after you've highlighted your best vertical explorations and have made plans to move them into different, cool, and creative mediums, it becomes time to build in some more dynamic connections. However, whereas with the micro-stories, you had room to build in six or more connections, with vertical explorations, you'll probably only have room for a couple.

Therefore, here's your mission: Take *one* of the six dynamic connections detailed in the previous chapter and use it to connect each one of your vertical explorations to either a different *micro-story* (not the one from which the vertical exploration is derived) or a *vertical exploration* of a different micro-story.

Again, your vertical exploration is already necessarily connected to its parent micro-story through plot, locations, and/or characters, so now we want to focus on dynamically connecting to other micro-stories in your macro-story timeline or their own respective vertical explorations.

For a refresher, the different kinds of connections at your disposal are:

1. Past-Plot Impact;
2. Future-Plot Impact;

3. Character Connections;
4. Location Connections;
5. Callbacks; *and*
6. Story Seeds.

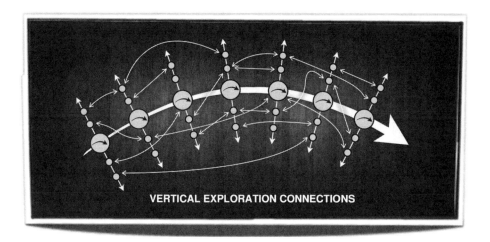

Just by looking at the vertical exploration connections, you really see the Rat King coming to life and this isn't even showing the dynamic connections between the micro-stories themselves.

We love the Midwest.

Let me take this opportunity to say that whereas the macro-story element of our campaign is more akin to a West Coast transmedia approach, the vertical exploration aspect of the campaign should appeal nicely to East Coast transmedia enthusiasts. We are now taking a single story (our micro-story) and extending it and spreading it in meaningful, additive ways into multiple mediums. At the end of this whole process, you'll have multiple self-contained East Coast transmedia projects that are all connected in a West Coast transmedia way and work together to tell one giant story.

We call it Midwest transmedia.

How awesome is that?

HERE'S A QUICK SUMMARY.

In some mediums, certain great scenes, sequences, or perspectives either can't be explored because of time, budget, page count, or some other creative decision and are left out of the final iteration of the project. However, through vertical exploration, the 360° Storyweaving Process revives these seemingly wasted narrative pockets and uses them to help market the stories from which they were cut.

Vertical exploration identifies all the narrative pockets that lie within the same narrative space and time of your micro-story and can be described as either narrative excess or another character's perspective. From that group, only the ones rewarding to the fans or additive to the micro-story are chosen to be vertically explored.

These pockets are intentionally not developed as fully as their micro-story counterparts and are left to rely on the micro-stories for full comprehension and context. They are merely slices of a bigger pie. They are then split off and separated from the micro-story and spread into a different medium from the micro-story, thus creating an additional point of entry into the project and helping pierce additional demographics for the micro-story itself.

In order to heighten intertextuality and crossover potency, limited dynamic connections are made between the vertical explorations and other micro-stories or other vertical explorations birthed from other micro-stories.

HERE'S YOUR HOMEWORK.

1. Go through each one of your micro-story treatments and identify at *least* four narrative pockets (consisting of either narrative excess or another character's perspective) that have the potential to be vertically explored.

2. Make sure the potential explorations are either additive or rewarding for the audience. If any of them aren't either, find a different potential candidate or build in an element of additive comprehension.

3. Develop it just enough to survive being separated from the micro-story, but make sure it relies on the micro-story for full comprehension and context.

4. Take each vertical exploration and spread it into a medium different than that of its parent micro-story. Remember, with vertical explorations your mediums don't necessarily have to be independent revenue generators and can be creative, out-of-the-box ideas.

5. Choose one of the six types of dynamic connections and connect each vertical exploration with either:

  • A different micro-story that *is not* the micro-story from which the vertical exploration was birthed; *or*

  • A vertical exploration story from a different micro-story.

CHAPTER NINE

SO NOW WHAT?

SOAPBOX, VIABLE SETTING, MACRO-STORY,
MICRO-STORIES, MULTIPLE MEDIUMS,
DYNAMIC CONNECTIONS, VERTICAL EXPLORATION

One-third congratulations.

If you're still with me, congratulations.

Your head probably hurts and you're more than likely exhausted due to the massive amount of information that's been thrown at you. Honestly, it's enough to fill an entire semester's worth of classes and it's definitely not for the faint of heart.

By now, you know how to build a thematic foundation for your project, create a viable setting that will spawn multiple stories for years to come, give your storyworld a structured arc, develop a variety of micro-stories to be spread into multiple mediums, dynamically connect all of them, and vertically explore all the additive and rewarding nooks and crannies to add even more depth.

It's big.

It's ambitious.

And you know what?

You're not done.

You've made great progress, but there's more.

I'm not joking.

Seriously.

While this is the only phase of the 360° Storyweaving franchise I'll cover in detail in this book, there are actually two other subsequent phases that are equally as dense and detailed. While these will be covered and broken down in other volumes, the fact remains you are only one-third finished.

This isn't to minimize what you've done. Not at all. You've constructed a massive, impressive, steely-strong, creative architecture that will stand the test of time and allow you to build on it for decades. That's awesome and is extremely rare no matter what part of the entertainment industry you're in.

But, again, you're only a third of the way home.

En la fase dos.

That means "on to phase two" for all you gringos out there, which includes myself (I admit I used Google Translate).

While I said I was going to detail the next two phases of the 360° Storyweaving franchise in their own books in order to give the topics their proper treatment, I'm going to go ahead and give you a brief explanation just so your head can start acclimating to the full scope of an entire campaign.

The second phase of our campaign is what we call the *Immersion Phase*. The focus of this phase, as you can probably guess, is to take all the creative architecture and the rich storyworld from the Creation Phase and build ways to completely immerse the audience in it and create a pervasive 360° entertainment experience. Gone are the days where audiences are content with only experiencing a television show's storyworld for forty-five minutes a week. Now, when those forty-five minutes are up, the audiences demand they be able to go to other mediums, other channels, and other components in order to continue their experience of the story and the storyworld.

The 360° Storyweaving franchise further immerses audiences into its storyworld through two major ways:

1. **Thematic Merchandising:** The focus of thematic merchandising isn't simply slapping a brand on a T-shirt. It's about making your world come alive through merchandising efforts. The primary mechanism for this is designing and offering the audience world artifacts from your project. I'm not talking about fossils, I'm talking about any objects or clothing that appear in your storyworld.

   For example, there's a big difference between buying a hat with *The Walking Dead* logo on it and buying the hat Rick Grimes wears in the series. What are those pieces of clothing or jewelry your characters wear that you can provide the fans the opportunity to attain? Can you manufacture pieces of art or decorations from your world? Thematic merchandising is all about reaching into your fictional universe, pulling out select pieces, and giving your audience the opportunity to physically hold onto them.

2. **Media Blurring:** The purpose of the Media Blurring component of this phase is to blur the lines between reality and fiction through the strategic use of various media components.

This will consist of constructing a comprehensive social media and web architecture for your creative components, including social media profiles for your characters, websites and blogs for any organization appearing in your stories, and billboards, print ads, and online promos as if your organizations and characters are real. Everywhere your fans look, especially online, they should find evidence that your storyworld and its respective characters may actually be real.

The creators of *The Blair Witch Project* put themselves on the map by expertly blurring the lines of reality and fiction. Notably, the producers of *Prometheus* released a TED Talk set in 2023 where cybernetics pioneer Peter Weyland speaks about his vision of the future. It was staged and promoted exactly like a real TED Talk and is a great media-based extension of the story.

Once you've built the immersion architecture, you can then run immersion stories and experiences with and across the architecture, such as Alternate Reality Games, for a greater level of engagement for your audience.

Time to build community.

You've created your storyworld from the ground up, mapped its narrative, and created your characters in the Creation Phase. Then, you formed a great strategy of how to further immerse your audience into your storyworld in the Immersion Phase. Now, it's time to turn your audience into a community.

In marketing circles, the terms *audience* and *community* are tossed around recklessly, making them seem synonymous. The problem is they're far from it. In fact, they're pretty much exact opposites. Think of the differences between a football team and the fans who watch the game. The football team is made up of players who work together and coordinate with each other to create common success. If they are unsuccessful, they tweak and work and are motivated to continue to generate that success.

The fans, on the other hand, are individual observers who have a similar interest in success, but aren't working together to generate the success. Fans help achieve success on some broad level (more fans means more ticket sales, which means a bigger budget to get better players or simply an intangible morale booster for the team) but they don't have the same unity as the team. Plus, when success isn't achieved, they'll stop coming.

A community will bridge the gaps between releases because the fire of excitement will continue to be stoked. While an audience will blast you on your Facebook page, a community will take up for you. When an audience will complain about price, a community will focus on why your project is worth it. Audiences only passively engage with each other (if at all), while community members actively engage with each other even when you're not directing them to. Audiences are good, but communities are so much better.

So, how do you build them?

Two ways:

1. **Online communities:** Building online communities for your project centers on actively engaging with your fans and incentivizing them to engage with each other. Interface with them through your website and/or forums, give them projects to work on together, have them create content themselves, have them brainstorm solutions to problems or encourage them to write fan fiction and use the stuff that's quality. Create human conversation and connection that most traditional entertainment franchises fail to achieve.

   As an aside, creating an engaged and participatory culture is one of the most important aspects of a transmedia project. While we haven't dealt specifically with engagement during the Creation Phase, you should always be thinking in these terms. Brainstorm ways of getting your fans involved early, even during your creative, development, financing (this is especially true if you're using crowdfunding resources to back your project), and even your production process. The more engaged and plugged in your fans are, the more likely you'll be able to form the community you need.

2. **Offline communities:** Building offline communities really goes back to the first thing we covered — your project's theme. Now that you have material, figure out how to literally go into your community and use the material to further your theme or purpose. For example, the Mattel franchise, *Monster High*, was meant to teach kids they didn't have to be ashamed of their differences. So, what Mattel did was partner with the Kind Campaign, which is an anti-bullying organization, and allowed the campaign to use its *Monster High* materials in schools as a means to teach this theme to kids. This really brings the project full-circle.

Start writing the franchise blueprint.

By the time you do all the homework assignments at the end of each chapter, you will have amassed quite a bit of creative output. Now it's time to start putting it all together in one, big document. Some folks call this document a bible, story canon, or a production guide, but we like to call it a franchise blueprint since it not only details and memorializes the creative canon of the storyworld, but it also outlines all the practical plans and strategies for the entire project, including functionality, marketing promotions, and social outreach initiatives.

Take every description, every story treatment, every connection, every character breakdown, every vertically explored story, every creative decision, every chart, every graph, every bullet point, and every immersion and community strategy you design in the second and third phases and lay it all out in a clear, coherent document. Collectively, it will all form the franchise blueprint.

Once finished, the franchise blueprint will help guide you and/ or others as you begin to write and produce the content. It will literally have everyone working on the project on the same page.

If a writer has a question about a story, it'll be in the franchise blueprint.

If a producer has to change a location in one of the stories, the franchise blueprint will tell him all the ways the change will impact the other stories.

If a fan calls you out on a continuity question, the franchise blueprint will tell you how to set him straight.

It'll act as a guide and a built-in project manager as your 360° Storyweaving franchise goes from development, to writing and implementation, to production and brand managing.

For our *City of Refuge* project, the first draft of our franchise blueprint was just shy of 150 pages. However, as the project grows and changes and we bring in more collaborators and partners, I expect it will ultimately be around 400 pages by the time we move into production.

Sure, it's hefty and takes a lot of work, but this is the document that will guide you and your teams through years of content creation. Looking at it that way, you can't expect it to be a handful of bullet points pasted on a Word document.

Once you have a healthy draft of the franchise blueprint, the vision of your project should be crystal clear to anyone who sets eyes on it. Communicating your vision and the depth of the project is one of the most important parts of gathering partners, investors, and collaborators, which makes your franchise blueprint one of the most valuable tools in your arsenal.

SOME PARTING WORDS.

And here we are.

Finally.

At the end of the book.

No more macros, no more micros, no more arcs or explorations.

Let me take a moment to compose myself...

Ultimately, you may need to read through this book a couple more times to fully absorb all the intricacies of the 360° Storyweaving approach. Regardless, I'm convinced I've given you the tools to truly create a quality narrative that is pervasive, participatory, sprawling, and most importantly, can withstand the rigors of being stretched and expanded for years to come. Accomplishing such a feat will automatically set you apart in a hyper-competitive entertainment landcape.

A great transmedia project may start with a single logline, but as you apply this 360° Storyweaving Process, and even put your own spin on the process, you'll be able to watch as it becomes a living, breathing entertainment experience right before your eyes.

Just remember, even though others may have more money, more experience, or better technology, it's your story that will allow your project to evolve and grow into something that will affect people's lives for decades. It's your story that will motivate fans to help you improve and refine your project as time goes on. It's your story that will hook them. If you don't have a great story, you're sunk, no matter how much engagement you provide, how many cool mediums you can take advantage of, or how innovative your technology elements are. The bottom line is that a great transmedia project is built upon the foundation of a great story.

And now you know the right way to build one.

CHAPTER TEN

SOME
SAGE
ADVICE

At this point, I know you feel like I've been talking to you for hours on end, but allow me to formally introduce myself.

Hi. I'm Houston.

Like the city.

Though, I was born in Ohio, grew up in Kentucky, graduated from college in West Virginia, went to law school in Virginia, and live in California.

Curious, I know.

A few things about me to get started:

- My full name is made up of three first names — Houston. Joe. Howard. For some reason, this has been the cause of an inexplicable amount of confusion for people throughout my life;

- I have a peculiar aptitude for creating board games;

- I have been called by some a "serial hobbyist," which seems to be the pejorative version of the preferable "renaissance man";

- I exploited a loophole in my undergraduate program and saved myself from a full semester of classes (a feat that I honestly don't get enough credit for — pun intended);

- It's possible I've heard the whole "Houston, we have a problem" joke well over two thousand times throughout my life;

- I love Cincinnati sports (Go Reds/Bengals!), but root for the University of Kentucky in basketball; *and*

- I'm a huge fan of timely and well-placed analogies.

I went to law school at Regent University School of Law in Virginia Beach, Virginia, and loved every bit of it. I never had the whole "I'm completely overwhelmed, I have no life, I'm drowning in a sea of briefs and dissenting opinions" feeling that so many law students have. Honestly, law school came easy to me. God helped me through and showed me how to do very well. Heck, I even won the Virginia Trial Lawyers award for the best blue chip, up-and-coming trial lawyer. Don't think I'm saying this to brag about myself — that would be rude.

I'm merely telling you this to set up what a big decision it was for me not to practice law, and instead, pursue a career in filmmaking.

The last semester of my third year, my wife and I began seriously praying about what God needed us to do for the rest of our lives and shockingly, it wasn't being a lawyer. Not that my degree was a waste by any means. Thankfully, a Juris Doctor is a wildly versatile degree. We simply examined what we would do if we had all the money in the world and failure was out of the picture. For me, it was making movies. I could do that all day, every day and it would never feel like work. So, we sold everything we had, packed what we could in our Jetta, and drove to Los Angeles.

The only problem was that when we arrived to the sunny West Coast, I realized I didn't *really* know how to do anything. I mean, I had a good idea of what to do, but the difference between having a good idea of what to do in the film industry and really knowing what to do in the film industry is as a big as the Grand Canyon (which we saw on our cross-country trek).

So, I was left with a decision: go to film school and incur another round of student loan debt or spend a couple hundred dollars reading books. Lots and lots of books.

I chose the books.

I went to the bookstore and devoured every film book I could find — producing books, writing books, directing books, dialogue books, character development books, production management books. Interestingly enough, I began to notice that all the books I gravitated toward had an MW logo on the spine and before you know it, I was brand-loyal to Michael Wiese's line.

William Indick's *Psychology for Screenwriters*, Stanley D. Williams' *The Moral Premise*, Paul Chitlik's *Rewrite*, William Akers' *Your Screenplay Sucks*, Pamala Douglas' *Writing the TV Drama Series*, Jennifer Van Sijll's *Cinematic Storytelling*, Tom Malloy's *Bankroll*, Maureen Ryan's *Producer to Producer*, Blake Snyder's *Save the Cat* series, Martin Roth's *The Writer's Partner*, and Christopher Riley's *The Hollywood Standard* became just a select few MWP books that acted as my film school curriculum.

When I decided to write *Make Your Story Really Stinkin' Big*, I only sent it to one publisher. When MWP decided to make it part of the very same line that helped me get started in the industry, I was stoked — and honored — and humbled to be in the MWP fraternity with so many capable industry professionals.

However, even after filling my head full of industry knowledge, it was still tough to find a footing. Hollywood is a competitive place. Not literally Hollywood the city — it's just kind of dirty and weird, but "Hollywood" the industry. Tens of thousands of scripts are registered with the Writers Guild every single year. Every day studios and agents are bombarded with every idea, concept, and pitch imaginable — all from really smart, capable people who were probably the most artistically-gifted folks from their hometowns. Literally, you have 50,000 crazy-talented people all running for one doorway.

Trust me, it's bananas.

I don't say this to scare you away from the industry. Not at all. For me, quitting was not an option. I was called here for a reason, so I'm staying until I achieve everything I'm supposed to achieve. However, that doesn't mean I had to follow the giant herd of people running for that one, lucrative doorway inside the industry. And you don't have to either.

For me, I chose (and am still choosing) to sneak in through a side window by thinking slightly differently. I didn't just go by the industry's status quo. Instead, I looked at where culture and media were heading. I looked at the shift that is happening in how audiences consume content and the democratization of content creation. I saw how new, interesting distribution channels were popping up and I endeavored to be a Swiss Army knife rather than a machete.

Enter 360° Storyweaving.

This process has allowed me and the team I've assembled to not only continue to develop content in the area that's closest to our hearts (film), but it's also allowed us opportunities to navigate a competitive industry in a recessive economy. It's led us into not just meeting with studio heads and independently pursuing our own productions, but also into helping other people and companies with their projects through consulting and partnership. Also, it's allowed us to expand in ways we never dreamed of, such as using our 360° Storyweaving process to facilitate corporate branding initiatives and work with school systems on both getting literature-averse students to love to write, and overhauling their writing standards.

This process has diversified us brilliantly so we can now leverage our success in the education space to get meetings with producers and then use our success in the film space to get meetings with potential corporate clients. It really has been a cool journey.

So, while so many people will tell you that it's folly to pursue a career in entertainment (especially in the current economy), I say simply do what you were put on this planet to do and don't let outside influences sway you from your path. If that's not entertainment, but you want to try the entertainment industry anyway, you'll more than likely burn out within a couple of years.

But if it is entertainment, know that you really need two things to complement your talent: perseverance and the ability to understand the times in which we are living. I can't teach you to be talented and I can't teach perseverance, but I'm being truthful when I say this book can help with the last one.

People are changing. The economy is changing. The industry is changing. We're living in a time where marketing, technology, and entertainment are merging like never before.

Therefore, as professional storytellers, we need to stay light, efficient, and versatile in the way we communicate with audiences. As people who need to make car payments and pay rent, we also need to find new, interesting ways to break into the industry and actually be able to do what we love for a living and not just as a hobby.

I truly believe this book can help you do just that.

So, go ahead and get to work.

Seriously.

You don't have all day.

ABOUT THE AUTHOR

Houston Howard is the CEO/Founder of One 3 Productions. He is a recognized leader known for crafting strategic vision used to achieve business and creative goals. Houston offers a unique blend of executive acumen and creative ingenuity to the leadership role. Since the company's formation, Houston has aligned it, internally and externally, with his strategic vision of the future.

Creatively, Houston is responsible for shaping the overall makeup, development, and direction of the One 3 Productions creative team. Additionally, Houston is the main screenwriter for the team as well as the lead board game developer. To date, Houston has overseen the creation and development of the company's first transmedia franchise *Fury*, in which he designed the board game, wrote the feature film script, and was the creative director for the rest of the universe. Additionally, Houston is currently the creative director and head writer of the independent transmedia franchise, *City of Refuge*.

In addition to his film experience, in which he wrote and produced the independent film *Artificial Red* and produced the weekly thirty-minute television broadcast *Shaking Foundations*, Houston has created and designed multiple independent board games.

He also attended law school, where he specialized in entertainment law and trial advocacy and was awarded the 2005 Virginia Trial Lawyers Award upon graduation.

Houston currently resides in Burbank, California, with his fetching wife, Courtney, and their spunky canine companion, Lucy.

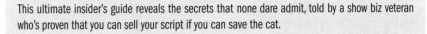

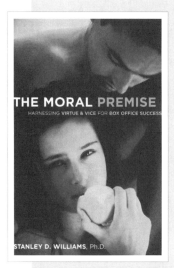

THE MORAL PREMISE
HARNESSING VIRTUE & VICE
FOR BOX OFFICE SUCCESS

STANLEY D. WILLIAMS, Ph.D.

This book explains how the moral premise – a statement of truth about the protagonist's psychological predicament –is a fundamental part of every successful movie's structure. It is also a book about how you, the filmmaker, can appropriate the moral premise to create great motion pictures that resonate with large audiences.

You will learn:
· The history and theory of the moral premise
· Its components and structure
· Its use in creating remarkable character arcs, act breaks, turning points, and dramatic beats
· A step-by-step method for embedding a true moral premise into a three-act screenplay

Understand and embrace one of the most fundamental structural aspects of storytelling, the basis for the most popular movies of all time. Use what has proven to be successful to create your own success and – in the process – entertain, delight, challenge, and uplift this generation and the ones to come.

"Insightful, thoughtful, and unique. I wish more people were writing the kinds of things Stan is writing. It's a much needed, fresh approach to the art and craft of writing."
> – Ed Solomon, screenwriter, *Levity, Men in Black, Bill and Ted's Excellent Adventure*

"A very interesting look at storywriting for the screen or novel. A great overview of how to structure a story."
> – Howard Kazanjian, producer, *Star Wars: Return of the Jedi, Raiders of the Lost Ark, Demolition Man*

"Stan Williams' book does what an undergrad and graduate education in film could not: Distill what makes a movie "good" into a concise, workable theory that guides every scene."
> – Jim Rossow, screenwriter, *Hijacking Hollywood*

STANLEY D. WILLIAMS is an internationally award-winning filmmaker, writer, and instructor. During the past 30 years, he has produced, written, directed, shot, or edited over 400 projects.

$24.95 · 219 PAGES · ORDER NUMBER 56RLS · ISBN: 9781932907131

YOUR SCREENPLAY SUCKS!
100 WAYS TO MAKE IT GREAT

WILLIAM M. AKERS

All beginning writers make the same mistakes — and many "pros" do, too! Because nobody in Hollywood will give your script a second chance, it better be perfect the first time out. No longer will you worry that a producer or story executive will toss your script in the garbage at page fifteen because *Your Screenplay Sucks!* Akers' checklist will eliminate all the flaws in your screenplay, guaranteeing a cover-to-cover read.

This book includes the most comprehensive checklist of fatal errors all writers make — and then provides the tools to fix them.

In today's highly competitive story market, this is the only book that finds the flaws in your script — like a heat-seeking missile — and shows you how to eliminate them.

"William M. Akers is a renaissance man of film who is at once a big studio writer, independent writer/director, and caring, insightful teacher. He also knows every trick in the book when it comes to fixing a script. And this is that book! A must for any writer facing 'the dark night of the script.'"
— Blake Snyder, author, *Save the Cat!*®, *Save the Cat!*® *Goes to the Movies*

"Don't even think about writing a screenplay without reading Your Screenplay Sucks!!"
— Linda McCullough, Columbia College Chicago

"A book about screenwriting that reads like a good screenplay. It is so full of great stories, examples and advice that I couldn't put it down."
— Tom Schulman, Academy® Award-Winning screenwriter, *Dead Poets Society;* screenwriter, *Honey I Shrunk The Kids, What About Bob?*

A Lifetime Member of the Writer's Guild of America, WILLIAM AKERS has had three feature films produced from his screenplays. A writer/producer with 15 years experience, he has written feature scripts, series television, and documentaries for MGM, Disney, and Universal, as well as the Fox, NBC, ABC, TNN television networks. He received a Telly Award for directing and producing non-broadcast documentaries. He teaches screenwriting and filmmaking at Vanderbilt. His feature film, *105 Degrees and Rising*, about the fall of Saigon, is in pre-production.

$19.95 · 220 PAGES · ORDER NUMBER 85RLS · ISBN 13: 9781932907452

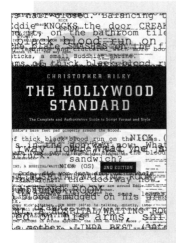

THE HOLLYWOOD STANDARD
2ND EDITION
THE COMPLETE AND AUTHORITATIVE GUIDE TO SCRIPT FORMAT AND STYLE

CHRISTOPHER RILEY

This is the book screenwriter Antwone Fisher (*Antwone Fisher*, *Tales from the Script*) insists his writing students at UCLA read. This book convinced John August (*Big Fish*, *Charlie and the Chocolate Factory*) to stop dispensing formatting advice on his popular writing website. His new advice: Consult *The Hollywood Standard*. The book working and aspiring writers keep beside their keyboards and rely on every day. Written by a professional screenwriter whose day job was running the vaunted script shop at Warner Bros., this book is used at USC's School of Cinema, UCLA, and the acclaimed Act One Writing Program in Hollywood, and in screenwriting programs around the world. It is the definitive guide to script format.

The Hollywood Standard describes in clear, vivid prose and hundreds of examples how to format every element of a screenplay or television script. A reference for everyone who writes for the screen, from the novice to the veteran, this is the dictionary of script format, with instructions for formatting everything from the simplest master scene heading to the most complex and challenging musical underwater dream sequence. This new edition includes a quick start guide, plus new chapters on avoiding a dozen deadly formatting mistakes, clarifying the difference between a spec script and production script, and mastering the vital art of proofreading. For the first time, readers will find instructions for formatting instant messages, text messages, email exchanges and caller ID.

"Aspiring writers sometimes wonder why people don't want to read their scripts. Sometimes it's not their story. Sometimes the format distracts. To write a screenplay, you need to learn the science. And this is the best, simplest, easiest to read book to teach you that science. It's the one I recommend to my students at UCLA."

— Antwone Fisher, from the foreword

CHRISTOPHER RILEY is a professional screenwriter working in Hollywood with his wife and writing partner, Kathleen Riley. Together they wrote the 1999 theatrical feature *After the Truth*, a multiple-award-winning German language courtroom thriller. Since then, the husband-wife team has written scripts ranging from legal and political thrillers to action-romances for Touchstone Pictures, Paramount Pictures, Mandalay Television Pictures and Sean Connery's Fountainbridge Films.

In addition to writing, the Rileys train aspiring screenwriters for work in Hollywood and have taught in Los Angeles, Chicago, Washington D.C., New York, and Paris. From 2005 to 2008, the author directed the acclaimed Act One Writing Program in Hollywood.

$24.95 · 208 PAGES · ORDER NUMBER 130RLS · ISBN: 9781932907636

THE MYTH OF MWP

In a dark time, a light bringer came along, leading the curious and the frustrated to clarity and empowerment. It took the well-guarded secrets out of the hands of the few and made them available to all. It spread a spirit of openness and creative freedom, and built a storehouse of knowledge dedicated to the betterment of the arts.

The essence of the Michael Wiese Productions (MWP) is empowering people who have the burning desire to express themselves creatively. We help them realize their dreams by putting the tools in their hands. We demystify the sometimes secretive worlds of screenwriting, directing, acting, producing, film financing, and other media crafts.

By doing so, we hope to bring forth a realization of 'conscious media' which we define as being positively charged, emphasizing hope and affirming positive values like trust, cooperation, self-empowerment, freedom, and love. Grounded in the deep roots of myth, it aims to be healing both for those who make the art and those who encounter it. It hopes to be transformative for people, opening doors to new possibilities and pulling back veils to reveal hidden worlds.

MWP has built a storehouse of knowledge unequaled in the world, for no other publisher has so many titles on the media arts. Please visit www.mwp.com where you will find many free resources and a 25% discount on our books. Sign up and become part of the wider creative community!

Onward and upward,

Michael Wiese
Publisher/Filmmaker